THE MEANING OF LIFE
FOR A MODERN MUM

To Di with love Di xx

THE

MEANING OF LIFE FOR A MODERN MUM

Di Turner

Matador
9 Priory Business Park,
Wistow Road, Kibworth Beauchamp,
Leicestershire. LE8 0RX
Tel: 0116 279 2299
Email: books@troubador.co.uk
Web: www.troubador.co.uk/matador
Twitter: @matadorbooks

ISBN 978 1785892 561

British Library Cataloguing in Publication Data.
A catalogue record for this book is available from the British Library.

Printed and bound in the UK by TJ International, Padstow, Cornwall
Typeset in 11pt Aldine401 BT by Troubador Publishing Ltd, Leicester, UK

Matador is an imprint of Troubador Publishing Ltd

I dedicate this book to my wonderful family.

To my husband, my soul mate, for being you and for being patient and understanding through the search for my meaning of life.

To my wonderful children who I love so much, you are my world, always be yourselves and live your dreams.

To my Mum for always being a fighter, you are so brave and strong and have always been there for me, enjoy life.

*Over the decades women have gone from being 100% Mums;
fought hard to be successful career women, who then hardly had any
time for being a Mum and now in the 21ˢᵗ century, women want
and need to be able to do it all; but how can we?*

Contents

Prologue

A Cup of Tea

How I'd love a cup of tea!
Hot, not cold.
How I'd love a cup of tea!
Not rushed.
How I'd love a cup of tea!
When I want it, not an hour later.
How I'd love a cup of tea!
Sitting down, reading a book
Or just staring into space, stress free.

If I can't even manage to drink a cup of tea when I want to and when it's warm, how on earth will I achieve my lifetime ambitions and bring up my children? How can I be the Mum I want to be?

A Bit About Me

Hi, I'm Di and I'm now 47 years old, however this book has been written over the last seven years of my life so my age ranges from 40 upwards through the different chapters. Oh to be 40 again! Or even 30 for that matter! Life really does fly by too fast. This book has snippets, insights and stories of life as a modern Mum, the fun, the struggles, the laughter and the pain. It has been a kind of therapy for me to write my experiences of juggling work in the high pressure corporate world with looking after my children. Trying to be the best at everything I do and most importantly the best Mum I can be.

I have lived in the same village in the Middle of England for most of my life. We have the national office of a major blue chip global company (Mars UK) on our doorstep and I have had a successful career with them for the last 22 years.

I met my soul mate when I was just 19 and we married when I was 29, having enjoyed ten years of travelling, partying, FUN and building our corporate careers.

My career soared at the start, with rapid promotions from forecasting to project management and to Export Manager, which was my dream job. Then, at the age of 31, I had my first baby and I knew I couldn't go back to working full time and be the Mum I needed to be. I didn't have a baby to never see him! So I compromised on both, my career and being a Mum, and went back to work part-time.

We now have two wonderful children, a son and a daughter and I work part time so surely I have it all! I am very lucky and people often tell me this so why do I have an inner voice wanting and needing more? Wanting it to be different? Wanting to be free from the juggling, free from the rat race, free to be me!

What is the point of it all? There must be more to life than this! I need to fulfil my dreams which include being a great Mum and being there for my children, always having time for them but also to live – REALLY LIVE!

What is the Meaning of Life for a Modern Mum?

In this book I have capsulized into chapters my experiences of the challenges, joys, frustrations and completely off at a tangent incidents that I've faced as a working Mum with huge expectations of myself. My journey has brought me to the conclusion that I need to chill more, move my needs up from the bottom of the list, break free from the ties of the corporate world and be the me I know I can be.

I hope you will find my book thought provoking and by joining me on this journey you too find your ideal work/life balance and your meaning of life.

Part One

Introduction

The Meaning of Life

The moment I gave birth to my first child I knew this was it; the meaning of life! My life would never be the same again and I was so glad. I had wanted a significant change in my life for some time but I really didn't realise just how big this was!

Am I an old Mum? Well, put it this way, when I was in hospital having my second baby at the age of 35 and the new Mum a few beds down was 18, I suddenly felt old and realised that I could have been her Mum and that must mean that there are some Grandmas out there the same age as me. Although it seems much more common these days to start having babies in your mid to late 30's, so in today's world I'm probably 'normal'. There are so many of us who have been building our careers, focussing on achieving that pinnacle of our working life before starting a family. Then when we do decide to start trying, it can take longer to conceive. Having been so in control of your career and your life all of a sudden you can't just get pregnant because you've decided it's the right time. You become more conscious of your body clock ticking and what if you can't have a baby after all this? What is the point of it all then? I remember this desperate feeling month after month and this was when I first started writing, putting my feelings on the page made me able to think more sanely about life.

Chapter One

*What are the Advantages and Disadvantages
of Being an Older Mum?*

Advantages:

- I've already had a life!
- I actually got fed up of going out getting drunk! You
  know 'same old, same old!'
- I have more patience.
- The little problems/inconveniences don't matter as
  much as they used to.
- I'm not easily embarrassed anymore, which is definitely
  a good thing with children.
- I know what my priorities in life are; family first.
- I have spent the time building a career and now I'm
  in the position where I can do a great job, part time,
  without the added pressure of striving for promotion,
  who needs it when you have the greatest challenge of all
  time at home!
- I'm full of enthusiasm at each stage of my children's life
  and want to learn new things with them. I'm growing
  in and out of each phase with them – made bibs at baby
  stage, sewed beautiful party bags, took up riding, now
  we're getting into music big time!! YES that's it; I'll re-

teach myself piano, I'll learn the guitar, the Ukulele, what a great time we'll have. This is what I'm like at each new stage in their lives and I can't help myself so I might as well just fully indulge and see where it takes us.

- We have more money than when we were younger BUT see disadvantages on this one as well.

Disadvantages:

- Loss of freedom; mourning the life of holidays, lie-ins and parties, which I enjoyed for rather a long time. It comes as a complete shock that you can no longer do what you want to do, when you want to do it because no matter what anyone says, babies don't just fit around your lifestyle, they take it over and everything has to change. No matter how ready I thought I was, I really had no idea of the massive impact having a baby would have on my life.
- Can't go out and get drunk because I am a responsible mother and I have to get up early EVERY day.
- I'm exhausted! I hate to say it but I do think young Mums have more energy.
- I get all enthusiastic about their new stage in life, completely engulf myself in it and then what do you know, they've moved on!!!
- I now question the importance of things I used to take for granted, like working for a living. What living? It just takes too much of my valuable time!
- I'll want to retire before they've even left home.   M y Parents, their Grandparents, are older and I'm already

starting to experience that I will be looking after my parents while trying to look after my children as well. The 'sandwich generation'! Let's face it, if my daughter has her first child at 35, I'll be 70 before I'm a Grandma!

- The money seems to be sucked into a vortex with children. Clothes, food, equipment, toys, nursery, then they start school and you think it will get cheaper and easier, think again!! Lessons for this, that and the other, subs, dance, karate, bikes, computer consoles, games, musical instruments, the latest craze etc. etc. etc. And as for getting easier, suddenly parental responsibility comes into its own.

I don't see myself as a natural Mum. When I had my first baby I didn't have a clue what to do and I found everything so difficult and so time consuming. Just trying to get out of the house seemed practically impossible, my son would be sick or fill his nappy just as we were going out of the door. I wasn't getting any sleep because he had terrible colic. He was constantly sick so the cleaning up was never ending. I just couldn't get the hang of breast feeding so I ended up expressing to then feed him from a bottle (double the work and double the time taken) but I couldn't possibly just resort to bottle feeding because then I would have completely failed in my motherly responsibility of giving him my milk. I remember deep down that I just wanted to give him a bottle and stop breast feeding but the pressure to be the 'perfect Mum' was so intense and I was so lacking in confidence in my new found role that my self-esteem was at rock bottom. How could it possibly be so difficult to look after a baby, I'm a successful and confident business women, I have a wonderful and supportive husband and my parents are only a few doors away but, oh boy, how I piled the pressure on myself. I have to cope! I have to be able to do everything the way the books are telling me I should, I have already failed at breast feeding, now I must do everything else even more perfectly. I must cook everything fresh for weaning. Nothing came naturally to me and I felt guilty about everything that I thought I wasn't doing well. I think I am getting better at it as they get older although I am always questioning myself and challenging myself to be a better Mum. Being a Mum is a constantly changing job where nothing stays the same and no one tells you the job description, you just have to work it out for yourself and constantly adapt and adjust as your children grow and develop. I will probably just feel like I've got the hang of it when they leave home and then what will I do?

The one thing I know for certain is that this is my role for life now and I love being a Mum and I'm so proud of my children, I just want to be the best Mum I can be.

Did our grandmothers have a better quality of life than we do today? They had time for reading, sewing, writing and teaching the children practical life skills. Children were more involved in the day to day household chores. Are our expectations too high today? For the 'perfect' home and the 'perfect' family! Do we set ourselves too many unattainable targets? From the day to day routine lists to be completed to the lifestyle ambitions that we have.

Have we lost sight of the importance of time? The time when we can be together and enjoy each other's company, the time to think and reflect.

Aren't good manners, principles and the ambition to be

a good person doing something worthwhile more important than the desire for wealth?

Have we become a lottery nation, so preoccupied with the hope of winning that we don't look at improving the here and now of our lives?

Reality TV stars! Are these really the role models that we want our children to aspire to be? What has happened to our ambitions, to our desire to achieve through hard work and merit and by helping others? What has happened to our desire to just be good people, being proud of ourselves and our contribution to society and feel happy through the happiness that we can give to others. To be highly regarded in the community we live in rather than known for some obscurity that gets into the national press or on TV?

Nowadays we are spending our lives rushing everywhere, in our grandmother's day there was time to sit down and think, more time to treasure and appreciate what they had, they were calmer, more creative, thoughtful times. We have so much more now in terms of possessions but do we ever treasure what we have? Do we ever truly treasure our wonderful children? Back then there was much more family time during and after the family meal, doing chores together, playing games and making things. Every member of the family had an important role in running the home.

Some of it is down to state of mind, if you think you have no time, you don't have any and a lot of the rushing around that we do is really very unproductive. I am trying my hardest to be more relaxed, chilled rather than stressed all the time, to turn the pace down and enjoy life for all that it is.

Chapter Two

*Does Having Children Keep You Young
or Make You Old?*

When will there be any time for me? I have so often thought it and sometimes even said it out loud and then felt guilty for even thinking it let alone saying it. I spend all my time juggling kids and work in the exhausting schedule of being a working Mum and I am so determined to enjoy my precious time with my children that I make myself feel guilty whenever I moan about anything, even if it is just in my head. Where will I fit in all the music lessons, clubs, dance, gymnastics etc. and find time for me? There really are so many things that I would still like to do with my life!

I fully immerse myself in each phase of their lives; I can't help it, that's me! I can't do anything half-heartedly; I give my full commitment to everything I do. Right now I think that I can learn a new musical instrument with them, they are picking it up so quickly and it looks like great fun, we could become a band together! However, I am completely forgetting that I am not young and when you are young, learning new things is so much easier but I always think I can do it and always give it my best shot! Full of enthusiasm and drive to succeed in everything that I do and wanting my children to feel the same, I feel really frustrated when they don't make the most of things and get bored or want to give it up. Then I have to think back to my childhood and try to understand that children have to experience many different things before finding what they really want to do and it is OK to change your mind and no longer enjoy something that you used to enjoy when you were 5 years old. We all grow out of things and children are experiencing this all the time at a rate of knots. Having children has meant that I am constantly trying new things, having new experiences in life with my eyes wide open like a child and it is amazing. Having children has made me look at the world around me with a different perspective, seize the moment, enjoy it for what it is because it is all gone far too quickly. It often feels that having to work just gets in the way of those 'seize the moment' times, especially on a beautiful summer's day when the kids are off school.

I'm so proud of their ability to learn and when watching them in any performance it takes all my self-control not to cry, with pride and happiness of course. This seems to be a trait of being a mother, one that I couldn't understand before I had my own children and one that I can't help doing all the time now that I am a Mum. I absolutely love learning new things with them and when it comes to their school work, I am like a sponge; I just want to know more and learn more. I am constantly questioning whether I learnt all the things that they are learning when I was at school, have I just forgotten it all? Was I not paying attention in the first place or is their education actually wider reaching and more interesting? I wish I had the time that they have to learn but of course like all children they don't really appreciate it, education is one of those things that you can only really appreciate when you're older and that is a sad fact of life!

Time is so precious to me now that I question any time that I have to spend doing things that are not enhancing our lives or any time that I have to spend away from my children when I really don't want to be away from them. It is the dichotomy of being a Mum, the un-choosable choice, work and personal ambition versus being with my children. I really don't think I would be completely fulfilled without achieving at work but I want to be there for my children when they need me. I always feel I should put looking after my children before anything for myself including work or any personal goals; I have terrible feelings of guilt if there is any special school event that I can't go to and always try to arrange my work around being with the kids.

So does having children keep you young or make you feel older? I love the way we can just have full blown giggly fun together on a wonderful summer's day. Having water fights or playing in the snow in the winter or just saying silly things that make us laugh, real belly laughs. That reminds me of my youth and makes me feel young again, forgetting the stuffy inhibitions of adulthood for precious moments of fun. On the other hand, sometimes I think I'm losing my mind; is it because of trying to juggle so many different things with work, home and school or is it just a side effect of getting older? How many times have I just been upstairs for that *thing* that I so desperately need to get but now can't for the life of me remember what it was or even what I needed it for? I sometimes just feel so absolutely exhausted that I really think I can't carry on at this pace, my mind never stops racing ahead, planning, organising and worrying about whether I am being the best Mum I can be. Are they having the best education? Are they getting enough sleep? Can I fulfil my dreams? Are we good role models for them?

I just heard on the news that they may have found a cure for Alzheimer's – I actually felt really pleased because I'm convinced I will suffer from it if the last few years are anything to go by.

How I wish I could stop the clock. When you're younger you wish your life away. Being a bit older (although definitely not old!), I want to slow it all down – now don't you remember your mother saying that and completely not understanding at the time! I know this time of my life, with the children being young, will be gone in a flash and that's why it's so important to enjoy every moment and be with them when I can. Knowing this, I put even more pressure on myself and have terrible guilty feelings when I've had a moan about the lack of freedom, lack of me time and needing some peace and quiet.

I don't really know the answer to my question but maybe it's a bit of both, having children both keeps you young and makes you feel older because of being so exhausted so my conclusion is that I need to have more of the moments that keep me young and less of the stressful exhaustion, if that is at all possible.

Chapter Three

Shall I Cry or Shall I Scream?

I could have cried this morning; well I'll either cry or scream at the top of my voice *"I can't do this anymore!"*

After having the whole of the summer holidays off work we are now back at school and work. The summer holidays were a glorious, relaxed, fun time together and oh how I loved not having the day to day timetable and hassles of term time and work.

So now I'm back at work, the kids are back at school and I'm back to the jobs all evening and the hectic mornings. Last night I had to wash 2 loads because the kids are playing out on the field at after school club, which is fantastic but it's already muddy and they certainly don't have 5 of each piece of uniform so I need to get it washed and turned around ready to wear again for the next morning. I have to make the sandwiches; they can have school dinners but being a bit fussy they don't like a lot of the menu. Also I'm not convinced that it is great food and it does add up (£3.60 per day for 2) if they don't even like it. My jobs are never ending…

I finish work at about 5.30pm and then pick them up from after school club, getting home around 6ish. Then it's non-stop; check for homework, reading diaries, notes from school, which always seem to be last minute requests for something urgently required the next day or an invitation to school to watch the children the next day or the day after. Can't they give us more notice? We do have busy lives! And I do need a bit of time to plan it into my work schedule as well as the after school activities schedule. Then I make tea, it'll have to be something quick again! Bath or shower time, milk and biscuits, followed by bed time which always ends up later than intended, quick stories, lucky if I'm back downstairs for 9pm. Now I'd really love to sit down and relax at this point BUT I need to make the sandwiches for the morning and get some washing done. The time I can sit down gets later and later… 9.45 pm last night.

6.45 am the alarm goes off and if my husband hasn't already gone to work at the crack of dawn, he'll bring me a cup of tea in bed which is a luxury and I do enjoy 15 minutes of calmly waking up and drinking tea, that's heavenly to me. Then up and at it! Washing into dryer, sandwiches into lunch boxes, make breakfast, get their clothes out ready, nag the kids not to fight, nag the kids to get ready, get into the shower myself, nag kids again to clean their teeth and get dressed because we must go in 10 minutes. Quickly get myself ready, I'm lucky if I have 5 minutes for makeup, if not, just slap it on quicker. Tussle with my daughter over brushing her hair and tying it back, my hair's still wet, never mind it'll dry on the way to work. Shout again, *come on now, time to go!* Shoes on, coats on, I fly down the stairs. The kids always do the last minute niggling at each other in the hallway (is that because I niggle at them all morning?), grab all the bags and we all get out of the door into the car. MADNESS!!!

I don't want it to be like this! I want calm mornings,

where we all quietly get ready. Is that possible? Is it actually my fault that it's all this hectic?

Why do I cry so easily now?

I cry for joy, pride, happiness, when the children are in plays, reading in church. I get upset far too easily at the slightest sad part in a film or song, I have even been crying while reading some Michael Morpurgo books as a bed time story. I didn't used to be this over emotional and I remember when I was younger seeing older women cry at weddings and thinking 'how silly!' Well it is a lot of the time but I just can't help it!

I was told that I couldn't take my 8 year old son into the ladies changing room at our local swimming pool. It was the cleaning lady who told me this in front of both of my children when they had just come out of their swimming lessons. I was very upset that they would think it's OK for an 8 year old boy to go into the men's changing room on his own, completely unsupervised. 'Very upset' is perhaps an understatement! I was so cross and upset at being approached in this manner and that she could possibly be telling me to put my son at risk that I burst into tears in front of her while we were having the discussion. This was a completely ridiculous situation and my poor son felt terrible but as I explained to him through my tears, it was absolutely not his fault, it's my duty to look after him and we will not be going to that swimming pool again!! I couldn't help bursting into tears again when I told my husband.

I will not put my son at risk so we will find another swimming pool with family changing rooms but then I still find myself worrying about the other 8 year old boys that might be going into the men's changing rooms on their own and are they safe? Let's face it, if you were a paedophile, swimming lesson time at the local pool would probably be a favourite! I just can't stop my mind worrying about things like this.

Is crying at the slightest thing normal (in any way)?

- Is it an age thing?
- Is it a being a Mum thing?
- Is it a tiredness thing? (Because let's face it, I've always been tired since having my first baby!)
- Is it all of the above?

I'd love to know whether other people are the same as me because sometimes I do think I'm going mad.

I asked my 8 year old son if he thinks I cry too easily. He said "yes, probably because you're lonely". I can't be lonely, can I? I never have a moment to myself. Is there something insightful in what he said? Is it the lack of real 'me' time where I can relax and be with others who don't depend on me?

I feel that I lost my freedom when I had children but I am now starting to question why I feel like that and is it because I try too hard to be perfect at everything and won't really accept help from others or let others do anything without me either re-doing it or feeling guilty that I didn't do it in the first place. Freedom has always been very important to me, I can't bear to be told what to do, to be dictated to or controlled in any way and yet when I really think about it now, I have let having children do that to me to an extent.

I have put everyone and everything at a higher point in the priority list than anything I need to do for me. I am now realising that I am the only one who can give me back my freedom by putting my own needs up the priority list. I have also realised that what I mean by freedom changes; as a child, freedom is being able to do something on your own, being allowed to go out on your own like being asked to go to the shop. Then in your later teens comes the freedom to choose what you want to do with your life and who you want to be with. Passing your driving test and having your first car is the ultimate first experience of real freedom, to be able to go where you want to, when you want to, no longer reliant on anyone else – I loved that feeling! Your first holiday with friends and not your parents, moving out of your childhood home. Getting a job to earn your own money gives you the freedom to choose what you do in your spare time.

Then you have a baby and all of sudden it is all turned on its head. You can no longer just go out whenever you want to or even just put your feet up and read a good book because now the baby needs you and dictates how your day is spent. Going on holiday becomes a whole new challenge. So now life entails going to work to earn the money to look after the children and pay the bills, including the very hefty mortgage required for a decent family home.

When you are paying for nursery and can occasionally grab some time off while they are in nursery, it feels great to experience a little bit of that freedom again but generally most of us don't pay for childcare unless we are actually going to work.

Then when the children go to school even more of your freedom is taken away because now you can only go on holiday during the school holidays, hence restricting you to the busiest and most expensive times for your precious, well-earned break.

I am on a mission to regain my freedom. Now that my children are older there are more things we can do together that can be fun, like going out for meals, going to the cinema, even shopping is more pleasurable than it was when they were younger. We can watch TV together and it can actually be something that I enjoy too. We can go on bike rides, go for walks in the countryside or just play at the park. I will also do things on my own and with my husband more, especially when the children are at friends' houses or staying with grandparents. I will be more relaxed about them having sleepovers and going for sleepovers and not feel guilty about doing things that I want to do. I am writing this while my daughter is at her gymnastic class, whereas I used to watch for the whole hour intently, always the dedicated, doting Mum, I am now using this time for me to read and write (I watch a little too), while she is enjoying herself doing what she loves, I am able to do the same and it's perfect.

Chapter Four

Is it Different for MEN?

This may seem completely stereotypical!
But YES it SO is!

My husband is great with the kids, great around the house (that makes him sound like a dog doesn't it – sorry), we do share things *BUT* I'm the one who always organises everything the kids need and everything that they are doing at school and out of school. I'm the one who deals with all the school letters. I'm the one who knows what they need for school the next day. I think this is all fairly typical and of course all my fault because would I really have it any other way?!

The thing that men seem to be able to do so well is keep a life for themselves. They have plenty of 'me time'! They (I am obviously referring to all men now – or certainly the majority) pop out whenever they want to whereas for me and most women, we have to organise the kids before we can 'pop' out anywhere without them. I do find it very frustrating to have to ask whether he can look after the children because I want to pop to the shops without them once in a while. I would love to just disappear for a walk or a bike ride or to visit a friend without the kids in tow – I should do it but it always seems more hassle than it's worth. There's always too much to do anyway, if I've been at work all day, I have to get everything ready for the next day, if I've been off all day, I suppose I feel I shouldn't need more me time – BUT I DO!

I just read on one of those parenting websites that recent research shows that men today are spending on average an extra hour per day with their children than they did 25 years ago and it is announcing it as though it's a major breakthrough, a wonderful achievement! Hurrah for the men for doing so well! I truly don't understand the women that take this crap seriously as though this is good enough. Surely parenting is a partnership and although most Mums, like me, are their own worst enemy because they just can't let go and have to be in control of everything when it comes to bringing up the kids, men should at least be there to help and be involved in this whole partnership and it shouldn't be a chore that we say well done for doing! When did we ever get a well done for being a good Mum?

Many couples don't engage in real, open and honest communication about their need for 'me time' or their feelings and their guilt for wanting more time for themselves. The competition between husband and wife for the time to do the things they want to do can be very destructive to the relationship especially when it feels (as it inevitably does) that one party gets all the time they need while the other looks after the kids. Does never being able to do what you want or need to do eat away at the foundation of your relationship? Is this the reason why more and more seemingly 'ideal' marriages are breaking up? Are couples completely forgetting the importance of spending time together as a couple because they are so busy with the 'tag-team' parenting that they never really see each other from one day to the next, let alone talk. Sometimes it seems like couples splitting up is becoming an epidemic. Women realising the benefits that they can get from being a single Mum, they will actually get some real 'me time' while the kids are with their Dad but there are obviously lots of disadvantages too, not least of which losing the man you love or must have loved once and probably would again in a less pressurised situation. There are so many pressures that go with bringing up children it would put a strain on the most perfect relationship and that is why it is so important to understand that none of us are perfect and no relationship is perfect and there is always something that could tip any one of us over the edge. The edge certainly seems closer when you are tired from lack of sleep, never have any time and just can't keep on top of the endless jobs.

From my experience when you add on top of this already exasperating situation any financial problems or illness or both, the slightest additional niggle could push you over the cliff edge that you are just about managing to hold on to. Things can fester and be built up to be much worse than they really are when the only conversations you are having are with yourself. I have really learnt that my inner voice can be far too critical and the only way to stop it is to speak out loud. Always be true to yourself and be honest even though it's really hard sometimes. It takes all your strength and you need to be strong together as a partnership to survive the constant challenges of parenthood. We all experience difficult times and it's how we choose to handle them that shapes our future for ever. I'm pretty sure it'll be worth it in the end.

Chapter Five

Appearance – Grow Old Gracefully – Not Me!

I have always taken pride in my appearance, I like to dress well and always wear a little bit of make-up and do my hair but it seems to be getting harder! The grey hairs are taking over; I now need to dye my hair every 3 weeks because the grey roots are so obvious, in fact it's a white track instead of a parting. I need to take a bit longer getting ready to be happy with the way I look and then feel good about myself but that is really hard with two young kids and all the running around and work. Finding the time to dye my hair is harder than ever but there is no way that I'll go grey or white! Grow old gracefully – not me – I'm fighting it all the way! I always remember feeling like I had an old Mum because she had grey hair and looked older than most of the other Mums and my Mum always succeeded in embarrassing me in public, mostly because of her pride in her children but head hanging embarrassment for us. She never seemed to know what was OK to say and what definitely wasn't OK to say in front of others. I don't want my children to feel like that, I want them to be proud of their Mum, of how I look and how I behave with them and their friends so I try my hardest not to be an embarrassing Mum. Although as I'm sure you can predict by this book, I probably will be a typical embarrassing Mum

– there's just no escaping it! No matter how young I feel inside, I am not young and I'm sure my children will remind me of that often when I don't understand the latest trend or don't like the right music or use old fashioned words. So I can now understand better how difficult it is for Mums and generally we do not intend to be embarrassing for our children, it just comes with the job!

My hair is naturally dark brown but with my roots so white now, I decided it was time to go lighter and had caramel blond highlights all over which I thought looked OK and even decided that I might as well go blond. I've been dark all my life and had that secret desire to try blond but never dared, well why not give it a go I thought to myself, hey, you never know I might have more fun too! It was a disaster but I kept trying to convince myself that it was OK, then I caught a glimpse of myself sideways in a shop mirror and realised once and for all that it just wasn't me! It was as dry as straw and had a similar appearance, in no way attractive and a complete waste of money. I'll chalk that one down to experience with a big note to self to never try that again.

I used to dress quite sophisticatedly for work but since having kids everything must be machine washable – dry clean suits are no more! I rarely wear a skirt because it isn't very dignified when you need to crouch down to help the kids with something when dropping them off or picking them up. I love my jeans now, not for work obviously but generally trousers and a top.

I have started to notice more wrinkles appearing around my eyes, forehead, mouth and my neck looks old at some angles, this seems to have happened all of a sudden and I even started to think maybe I would consider cosmetic enhancement like Botox, having thought when I was younger that I would never do it. Then at the age of 43, lumps suddenly started to grow around my lips under my very old scars, when I say suddenly, I really mean it, I woke up one morning and felt a lump had appeared. I kept thinking they would just go away on their own as quickly as they had come but after a couple of months my husband said you really ought to see the doctor about those lumps. Sometimes it takes someone you love to make you realise that you can't just leave it. I had been really worrying about what was happening to me. The 2 lumps were the size of peas and really hard, right underneath my existing scars around my lips making them protrude and look much worse. I went to my GP and his first suspicion was skin cancer so he referred me to a dermatologist immediately. After a week had gone by and I hadn't received the appointment I decided to go privately because the worry about it being cancer was awful. My GP had said the consultant would probably take a biopsy of the lump and this was really worrying me as well because I suffer with keloid scarring and any kind of incision no matter how small could then grow into a keloid scar.

I saw a consultant privately and he was fantastic. He immediately diagnosed the lumps as spontaneous keloid scarring, although he had never seen such an occurrence 30+ years after the original trauma and he started treatment immediately. I had to put steroid tape on the scars above the lumps every evening for 12 hours over an 8 week period to soften the lumps so that he could then inject steroid straight into them. After the first steroid injections I looked like I had a 'trout pout' and my lips were completely numb for a couple of days, then when the swelling had gone down I could feel that the lumps were a bit smaller and a bit softer. I carried on applying the steroid tape for the next 8 weeks, even through my summer holiday, until I was due for the second steroid injections which worked amazingly and now my scars are pretty much back to how they used to be. I am so grateful to my wonderful consultant and I have learnt my lesson to appreciate what I have and I wouldn't now consider any form of cosmetic surgery purely because of the ageing process. I am grateful for my face to be lump free and just have the scars that I have grown used to over the years.

Never mind, I suppose I have to admit it, I am now middle aged whichever way you look at it, at least my body is and it has been through the mill a bit. I need to accept that I will gradually look older. Although I do slightly mourn the passing of my younger years I look forward with excitement to the years ahead and the freedom that can come with older age and my better understanding of myself. Inside I will always be young.

Chapter Six

In Another World – My world!

Do you ever walk around and feel as though your mind is in another world? Sometimes I feel like I'm in some kind of bubble, I'm not really with it and I feel very laid back but completely ineffective in any task I try to do. Everything seems very slow but serene. Is it because I have so much going on in my mind that sometimes I shut it all out? Or is it just tiredness? Is it age? I don't know but it's very strange. It's like the volume and pace of life get turned down and I'm in my own little world for a while.

I can't believe what I did today! The kids and I had a very lazy morning (in my serene world today). We're on school holidays so not rushing anywhere but we do need to do the food shopping. Managed to leave the house at 11.30 am – shocking, I know! Then about half way to the supermarket (a good 5 miles), I suddenly remembered that I had left the back garage door wide open and the door into the house unlocked. I can't even use the excuse that I was in a rush! I turned the car round and went back to lock up properly. Then we set off again, finally getting to the supermarket at 12.30 and so decided we better have lunch first and then do the shopping. MADNESS!

Shopping with the kids is just such a nightmare! Can I have this? Can I have that? Can we go now? I wish I didn't have to do the food shopping but I do because although I am an advocate of on line shopping, I can never remember to get everything I need in one go or I need something so desperately, all of a sudden, that we have to go to the supermarket and while we're there we might as well pick up the rest of the food, toiletries and cleaning stuff we need. I am completely rubbish at shopping and really hate it – must try harder to do it all on line!

Sleep or should I say lack of could be the cause…

I didn't truly understand the importance of sleep until I had my first baby. I never sleep well these days. Every night I feel like at some point I am either woken by the kids or just wake up because it has become a habit and then lie there in bed drifting off and waking up with all the thoughts of everything I need to do and everything that I mustn't forget to do going round and round in my head.

I was so tired the other night and I just couldn't sleep so I took 2 sleeping tablets at 3 am, I slept great for 4 hours but then felt like a zombie for all of the next day – so I won't be doing that again, I certainly can't write a day off like that, there's far too much to do!

The only time I really manage to sleep is when we are on a long family holiday, once I've relaxed and no longer have all the day to day routine to keep up with. Therefore the conclusion must be to have more holidays because they are really important for my sanity and general health. The only trouble being that family holidays are getting more and more expensive as the children get older and already class as an adult for flights at the age of 12 and an adult for Disney at 10!

Chapter Seven

Money vs. Time

As I get older I have definitely realised that more money isn't the answer to happiness. You really can't just buy everything for your kids, to give them the best upbringing they need you, they need your time, TIME IS MORE PRECIOUS THAN MONEY!

You could buy the best education in the world but would that make them the best person they can be? The happiest person they can be? Or just the best educated?

I want my children to grow up well rounded with an understanding of what is truly important in life.

I want to be there for my children, to be an influence, a role model, a person that they can and do turn to. I won't always have all the right answers but that's OK too because it shows that no one is perfect and we can work things out together.

When you really think about it you have to question the progress that women have made in the last 50 years. We wanted equality and yes absolutely we are equally as important as men, yes of course we should vote and yes we should be paid the same amount for the same job. But where in all of this did women really realise that what we were doing was taking away our rights as mothers. Now we have to hold down a job and manage the household and look after the children and no one has invented more time in each day to be able to do this. Yes I know we have the labour saving devices for washing etc. but there is no invention better than a Mum for looking after the children and with our time now taken for working as well, we are spread thinner than ever. Sometimes I really wish I had the courage to 'just' be a Mum and not try to have it all and I only work part time, how on earth must it feel for Mums working full time?

In my opinion we (women) have changed the world because by having careers and earning good salaries the knock on effect has been the rise in house prices so that now it is normal to need two good salaries to be able to afford an average family home. Do we need to lower our expectations for the perfect family home with all the mod cons? Because in the end is this really making us happy? Do we need the perfect minimalistic interior with the modern open plan kitchen and perfect, clutter free living area? Or would we all be a lot happier if we could just relax, have time together and stop worrying about presenting the perfect family with the perfect family home?

Can we lower our expectations or is it too late?

I'm not as excessively tidy as many people by a long way but as the children get older and the toys more numerous, smaller and lots of bits everywhere that never stay together in any kind of order, I do find myself getting really frustrated with it all. I have to keep saying to myself "I'll miss it when they've gone!" And that's the crux of it, this time with the children is precious and very short when you think of your entire life so we Mums should be able to give being a Mum the time it deserves.

Chapter Eight

Just a Big Kid at Heart

I'm such a big kid at heart and I love the way the children remind me of this when they beg and beg me to join them on the inflatable water slide or in the paddling pool. When they've got me started there's no stopping me. I shriek with enjoyment, all my inhibitions gone and I'm like a kid again – no thoughts of washing or housework just fun, fun, fun – oh we must do more of this!

This is why I absolutely love our family holidays, we have been going to Florida for the last few years. My husband and I first went when I was 21 and he was 22 because some of our friends had moved out there and had bought a motel. We have both loved everything about Florida from this first visit, to the many more that followed and now taking our children to the place we love is pure utopia. Every holiday is different but the main thing we love is the freedom to have fun, day in day out, whether at a theme park, in the pool or on the beach. I have to say for me a big dose of predictable sunshine makes me feel fantastic. So with all these factors weighed up, even though we should probably spend some money on the house and another holiday to Florida will be very expensive no matter how much you budget, I can't help but say, let's book it because we'll all have a wonderful time again. The little voice in my head is telling me to make the most of this time because before you know it the children won't be coming on the holiday and it'll be back to the two of us (which of course will be an awful lot cheaper, so we can save money then!).

I went to see Mama Mia at the cinema with a friend last night – WOW – that's it, I am going to enjoy myself like a kid again and what better excuse do you need than playing with your own kids! The next time we get the water slide or the pool out, I'll be there in my swimming costume no matter who's here! And that's a promise to myself <u>AND</u> I am going to bounce on the trampoline every day (weather permitting) – why do I have to add that? Kids wouldn't would they!

I am excited at the thought of being like the film, young, fun, lively, carefree. In fact it even made me seriously think about spending the whole of the next summer holidays on Daytona Beach in Florida. I really am a dreamer but where would we be without our dreams and these dreams make me feel excited, happy and alive just by having them. I'll always have my dreams because I am a dreamer but I am also impulsive and live in the here and now. I believe it is important to be positive and happy with what you have now. Yes, we should all have dreams but enjoy the pursuit of the dream as well, don't spend your whole life waiting to achieve it or one day you might look around and realise that time has gone! People who want more all the time can be too busy to have fun… Let's not have to schedule that fun time in! Let's be more spontaneous! Let's learn from our children!

I was talking to my son last night when he was thinking about what he might like to do when he grows up and I said to him that I have always had a dream, my dream

31

has changed constantly and that's fine because we are all growing our minds all the time. I remember I wanted to be a model, a designer, a multi lingual interpreter, have my own shop, be PA to Richard Branson, run my own business selling fantastic dribble and sick proof bibs but that were soft and looked great (I got close with that one!), making amazing fabric gift bags for kids parties and now I dream of being an author and living part of the year in Florida with it's gorgeous sunshine and beaches. Just thinking of the sun on my body makes me feel great, my joints stop aching and I feel alive. The dream of sitting on a balcony overlooking the sea in the glorious sunshine writing, that's my dream now.

Your dream can be anything you want it to be and it doesn't have to be constrained to what you can definitely achieve because it can change or evolve over time. Never be afraid to have a dream and never think that you can't change your dream because you've just grown out of it – that's fine, it's yours and nobody else's, to have and to hold, to keep or to change, just enjoy dreaming it and you never know one day it could come true.

I feel weird saying this and I don't know whether I've ever said it out loud before but I do believe in angels or at least I do believe that life carries on after death in some form. There is a part of our ancestors within us and I don't just mean in our genes, I mean in our knowledge and the way each generation knows more. My daughter has often come out with things that I don't know how she could possibly know and she seems wise beyond her years. My son will throw amazing challenges into what I may think is as clear as black and white and it makes me challenge my thinking. How I love them both, how I love their thirst for knowledge and ability to absorb new information, how I want to learn more with them. I want them to keep their easy going, fun loving, thirst for knowledge because it is so easily lost through adolescence and into adulthood.

Another film that had a profound effect on me was Benjamin Button, I was mesmerised (and not just because of Brad Pitt, although he is gorgeous!). It made me feel emotional and I was very quiet and thoughtful afterwards because I am so lucky, I have my true soul mate, my husband. We have been together since I was 19 and through all the ups and downs of growing up together, having the children and a few of life's challenges along the way we are still together and I cherish our love. We must live our lives to the full, cut out the unnecessary nonsense of day to day living because you never know what's going to happen. Enjoy the moment and don't be grumpy or angry because it's just a waste of energy and time. I will really try to be more relaxed about trivial issues that are not life or death problems.

Chapter Nine

Routine

Routine, I hate it! I love to be impulsive, do what I want to do when I want to do it. I eat when I'm hungry, sleep when I'm tired but when you have children they need routine so I have had to succumb to it but it doesn't come naturally to me. When I think about it, my Mum was never good at routine either but she always had time for us. I have been known to get so carried away having fun with the kids that I forget to make lunch or tea so we just have something quick and easy but do you know what, it's never really mattered that much and as long as I try to keep to a skeleton of a routine we can all stay sane and happy.

Anyway, how important is this strict routine? Is my belief of its importance just what I have read, been told, or seen on the TV? Is it yet another thing for me to feel guilty about because I'm not good at it? All these so called experts telling us what we should be doing all the time isn't very helpful when it's yet another thing for you to feel bad about because you can't do it as well as they can. We are all different, some people thrive from a strict routine and others, like me, find it completely stifling because it can take any chance of spontaneous fun away. Yes, I'm sure children should have a bed time but can't it be flexed at least by half an hour to an hour each way without really worrying about it. So what if the ice cream van turns up at completely the wrong time and we end up having pudding when our meal is just ready to eat. Do we all stress ourselves out too much these days about the importance of the ritual timetable for the day? In the old days did it depend more on the weather and day light than the clock? I remember that my Mum was always very relaxed about bedtime. Bedtime for us was when we were tired and because I always needed my sleep I would go up to bed before my brother and my sister when I said to my Mum that I wanted to go to bed. Obviously this worked pretty well and my Mum was quite strict in that this flexible bed time was only if we were behaving ourselves. Any nonsense or fighting and we would be straight to our rooms. I have pretty much the same rule but because I still need my sleep and go to bed at about 10 pm most nights I do really want them in their beds by 9 pm. My daughter is like me and needs her sleep so it isn't a problem, I can see for my son though that it is becoming more difficult and he'll soon be going to bed later than me, especially if he starts going to youth club regularly. There will be times when I have to stay up to pick them up and of course I do go out later myself occasionally but I can't do it night after night. I think this is another factor of being an older Mum because I really do need to get to bed at a reasonable time, I prefer going out early and coming home early, I will struggle when the kids start going to discos, concerts and nightclubs. It makes me sound like a terrible bore, I hope I'm not but I just don't have the stamina that I used to have. Having children later in life has taken its toll on my energy levels and now that they are heading towards their teenage years I am feeling it more than ever.

During term time when we have the routine of school, work and all the after school activities I have completely and utterly had enough by the half term break. I need the holidays and so do the kids, we use the holiday time to have a complete break from all this routine and don't do the after school activities either, even if they continue through the holidays. We would all rather do different things. I don't mind now when the kids declare they don't want to do an activity anymore and want to try something new because the only way to discover what you enjoy doing is to keep trying different things and I completely understand that they get bored of things after a while because I do too. I don't make them stick with an activity term after term if they are not enjoying it, I try to encourage them to see a term out if we have paid in advance but I no longer enter into long drawn out persuasion tactics or bribery if they really don't want to do something. There are enough things in life that they will have to do without making after school activities compulsory!

Chapter Ten

The Love Tug: Work Ambitions vs. Family Values

I am ambitious, I have constantly shifting dreams but the one constant is that I want and need to achieve something I am proud of in my life, something that makes my mark on this earth. But I will not be owned by a company to the detriment of my children and our family time together. I am old fashioned at heart and want to be with my children every step of the way. I want and need to see them growing and developing. I need to be a main guiding influence in their lives and to do this I need to spend significant time with them. I also want to be a great role model for them in every way and this does include success at work, to show them what I can achieve and teach them that the world really is your oyster when you're young and nothing is out of your reach. You can work hard to achieve your dreams but you must enjoy the work as well because every moment we have is valuable.

I am on the school committee which I don't really have time to do and am not able to give them as much time as I would like to but I need to be involved because my children spend so much of their life at school. I need to connect with that time and understand more about what they are doing and get to know the teaching staff better.

It is a constant tug of my time between work and family but the children will win every time.

Please let me find the energy to fulfil my dreams in some small way! But don't let me ever have any regrets about not being there when my children need me or not spending enough quality time with them.

I know they'll be grown up before I know it but having them later in life I also know that by the time my daughter goes to university I could be retired. Yes, that's it, then I'll have plenty of time but will I still have the energy? I just need to focus on this precious time with the children now.

I do 'only' work 3 days a week and have a great, fulfilling and very challenging job. The company I work for have great family values and good family friendly policies, for example: I have just had the whole of the summer holidays off work as unpaid leave. When they say yes to these requests I know I am very lucky and why would I possibly need anything else. I am very dedicated to the work I do but I suppose if I'm really honest I am a little bored of it. I've been in the same role, 3 days a week, since I went back to work after having my daughter and the trouble is that other opportunities for working 3 days a week at my level are zero. So I stay in the role that I have and do a very good job. I am challenged but the longer you stay in the same role with a big business the more you see the same cycle of 'business change' that you have seen before but can't say that without coming across as an old 'has-been' with no imagination or foresight, when in fact if experience was more valued we could make real progress!

I find that I get much more real satisfaction from watching my children learn and develop and by getting involved and learning new things with them. Some of the things they are learning I must have done at school but it's a really good refresher and inspires me to want to learn more. There is so much for me to learn and so much more I could do in my life.

If only I could understand myself better and what I really want!

On one hand I want the freedom to be with my children every moment they are not at school. To have fun together on bike rides, kicking leaves, making snowmen, playing silly games, just having fun with no time pressures. I don't want them to have to go to after school club or holiday clubs or childminders; I want to be with them. I don't want to feel guilty when I need to finish work early because I have to pick them up. I don't want to be at work wishing I was with them.

On the other hand, I do have ambition and we do enjoy the luxuries in life. Nice family holidays, days out to fun parks, regular trips to the cinema and meals out so I need to earn enough money as well.

I've worked long and hard to build my career which now means that I do have a fulfilling and challenging job but with this there is pressure as well as the reward of reasonable pay. I have a part time contract to work 3 days a week but the days I work are long, hard days and by the time I pick the kids up at 6pm I'm exhausted and have no energy left for fun with them. The kids are always built up to hyper point by the time I pick them up from after school club and their behaviour can be terrible and I can't help thinking that they don't behave like this when I've been looking after them. Maybe it's just because we are all exhausted and it's too late.

What have we done to ourselves? With our desire for a career we have created our own handcuffs for life. Then we resent our husbands because they can just carry on with their careers without the fact that they have had children really having any detrimental effect on their work. They don't seem to experience this constant guilt and tug of love that we do. When I say WE, I do realise that many women seem to manage perfectly well but equally as many must struggle in the same way that I do. Will we just run ourselves into the ground trying to be the best at everything and in the process forget to have fun or just not find the time for fun!

In my dreams…

I want to have some wild adventures.
I want to be running along the beach in the sunshine
– all four of us.
I want us to dance in the rain.
I want us to have FUN!

Chapter Eleven

Homework and Practicing

On the days that I work (Tuesday, Wednesday and Thursday), the kids and I don't get home until about 6 pm. By this time we are all absolutely exhausted and really don't have the energy and I don't have the patience left for doing homework, nagging about practicing musical instruments, even getting children to read is very hard when they're tired and you're tired too.

It's not working! We have just been to parents evening and we need to do more work at home, especially with our daughter, she hasn't settled back into school very well (she is the youngest in year 1 and won't be 6 until next summer holidays). She doesn't understand why she has to work while the reception children are allowed to play. One of life's tough lessons very early! So now I feel even guiltier, it's so hard to do the best for your children. There is so much pressure from school to do more and more work at home with them.

Now I'm thinking that I have to find a better solution to this, can I change my working hours so that I can pick up from school say on a Wednesday and work the extra hours on a Monday? The trouble is, I feel like I am always asking for more 'special' treatment at work, I already want as many of the school holidays off as possible because I want to be with my children and childcare is so expensive for two it's hardly worth my while working. Also in the holidays they want to be at home or with their friends or on holiday not carted to this club and that club or a childminder. It is a really hard juggling act because I do have a great job for a great company but my children have to come first! No regrets ever! I don't want to look back and think I've missed this time with them.

No doubt I will go round in circles about this dilemma for a while but it won't go away so I need to come up with a proposal at work.

Amazing! Yet again, when I went to my boss with a proposal for spreading my hours over 4 days rather than 3 (with no increase to the hours I actually work), he agreed. We both agreed to be flexible and I would fit my hours around meetings and he would have no problem with me flexing my time to be able to pick up the kids from school at least one extra day a week so I would only work one or two long days at the most with the rest of the hours spread out. I feel so relieved, I can't even begin to express how happy this has made me, everything about me needs this flexibility and I will be able to be my best both at work and at home.

Chapter Twelve

Losing my Mind

Have you ever thought 'that's it, I'm definitely losing my mind!'?

This week has been manic and it's only Wednesday night. Snow started falling on Sunday late afternoon and by Monday morning there was a really thick covering, it was still snowing and more forecast for the rest of the day. For the first time since my son started school (he's in his fifth year now – called year 4 because of reception being the first year – very confusing!) the school was closed. We didn't find out until we were at the door all togged up with our winter gear on and the sledge in hand, ready to sledge down to school and I was feeling pretty good that I had managed to get us all ready and find all the snow gear in time for school (even spare gloves, shoes and socks in bags). I felt quite deflated; the kids were elated, "YIPPEE! No school – the best day of our lives!" Well, now that we are all dressed up we might as well at least go to the village shop on the sledge. Then I decided to ring my friend, who has children the same age, to let her know and see whether she wanted to meet us at the shop so that the kids could play together in the snow. We had great fun sledging, snowballing, building snowmen, one of the best days of my life as well. A day of being out for hours, then in to get dry and warm before going back out again. Three times in all and each time I hung all the wet stuff on radiators and got it dry again ready for the next outing. I would normally have had a couple of hours for getting household jobs done – a bit of time for me! Then work for 3 hours, then pick up from school. This is my new arrangement with work but obviously it doesn't take into account when the school is closed because of snow.

Monday night and I need to get everything ready for Tuesday; clothes washed and dried, all outdoor stuff clean and dry, spare clothes, gloves, socks and shoes in bags ready to go. Make the sandwiches and clear the car because it has stopped snowing now so I'm sure school will be open tomorrow.

Tuesday morning. It hasn't snowed since yesterday afternoon, the roads look a bit clearer, school will definitely be open! I get on with the normal morning rush. Then a phone call, I can't believe it! School is closed again. I have to get to work today so I frantically call my Mum as I will need to leave in 15 minutes, always last minute! Thank goodness Mum lives only 4 doors away, may seem too close to some people but actually it is great having my parents close by to help and support on these sorts of occasions. After two quick phone calls I have Mum coming up to look after the kids and a neighbour with a 4x4 going to give me a lift to work. I rush out the door with my hair still wet (as always) reeling off instructions to Mum for lunch, not too many treats etc…

It felt good at work that I had managed to get in, some people hadn't so the office wasn't as hectic as usual, at least I will definitely be able to finish on time. I had several phone calls from Mum just checking on things that they should or shouldn't do and what they have done and what they have eaten. Managed to finish a little early and arrived home by 5 pm. Then I clear the car ready for the next day and make sure that I can move it off the drive because I really must drive my car tomorrow and school will definitely be open. I spend the next hour playing in the snow with the kids, building an enormous snowman and shovelling snow to make a barricade to protect us from incoming snowballs. Lots of kids from the street joined us and it was great fun. We get in, strip off the layers of wet clothes and I make tea while the kids relax and get warm in front of the TV. While the tea is cooking I make a start on the washing and make sure that the gloves and boots and coats are drying on radiators. After tea it's back to routine, bath, milk & biscuits, bed, then I make the sandwiches and get all the bags ready for the next day. PHEW! 9.30 pm, everything ready, I can finally sit down with a nice gin and tonic, I'm exhausted!

6.45 am Wednesday, my alarm goes off – here we go again, must get up, so much to do, must drive car today, will school be open? Yes, I'm assuming it must be, there has been no new snow since Monday afternoon. Must be ready early because I have to de-ice the car and drive on compacted, icy snow out of our road until I get to the main road where it will be clearer. I won't go in the school car park because it's on a hill and completely hazardous when there is a bit of ice let alone snow and ice, I would never get back out again. I plan to park on the road outside the school, I hate doing it but I have the tuba today (which my son is having lessons on at school) and when I've dropped off, I have to go straight to work so I just haven't got time to walk. We are out the door by 8.30, school is only 5 minutes away (by car) and starts at 8.50 so we're doing really well – yes! we made it to school and I arrive at work at 9.00.

I feel a fantastic sense of achievement that I have managed the last 3 days on my own. You might be thinking where is the husband all this time? And I have to say that I wished he had been here because he has a 4 x 4 which would have made the driving part a lot easier. He drove to Scotland for meetings with customers in the very early hours of Monday morning when it had only just started snowing here. He'll be arriving back tonight and I feel like I've done so well, surely he'll be impressed! I want him to be impressed, I don't know why but it's important to me that he sees me as a great Mum who can cope with anything.

When my husband arrived home he forgot to ring me to let me know that he could pick up the kids from a friend's house who kindly offered to have them after school (because I didn't get to work on Monday, I have to work later today). Anyway, I pick them up straight after finishing work, still negotiating the hazardous side roads in my little Fiesta. We arrive home to discover that I had accidentally shut the cat in the lounge this morning and the poor thing was clawing at the door when my husband arrived home and had had a small wee accident near the door – he (the cat) had obviously tried his best not to wee and I feel so guilty, the poor thing. Then later when it's time to make the sandwiches for the next day, I know I had a container full of grated cheese but I can't find it anywhere in the fridge, oh where is it? I'm exhausted and frustrated now and when my husband opens a cupboard to get a glass out, there it is! Am I going completely mad or what!? And I thought I was doing so well – what else will I have done?

Oh no! Now my daughter has just been sick, what will I do tomorrow?

Chapter Thirteen

I Hate That I'm so Fussy

These days people seem to spend so much time worrying and talking about kids being fussy and assessing why. "Of course it must be down to their mothers!" This is what TV programmes seem to be telling us all the time. Do you know what, I don't believe any of that, I genuinely believe that we are born with certain preferences and sometimes with real aversions to some foods and no matter what we do we cannot make ourselves like them.

I am the worst of fussy eaters and always have been. I was brought up in a house where my Mum and Dad ate everything. Mum was from a farming upbringing and made everything fresh and grew lots of fruit and vegetables. My upbringing was not unlike 'the good life' in terms of a high level of self-sufficiency when it came to fruit and vegetables, although my Mum and Dad did go out to work to pay the bills. My sister eats pretty much everything and seems to like everything but not me. I declared myself vegetarian at a very young age and didn't find it difficult because I don't like 'proper' meat, meat that you have to chew, I can't stand the texture of it, literally it makes me retch. I hate mushrooms for the same reason and any meat substitute that is made to have the same texture as meat. I also found it easy because I'm such a soft and emotional person when it comes to animals I couldn't bear the thought of eating them. Mum says that one day we walked past a butchers shop and something that still resembled the animal was hanging up and that was the last straw for me, oh along with beef being served at an Auntie and Uncle's house that had actually been a cow I knew by name on the last visit to them.

My brother, being younger than me, tended to follow my lead a bit and that infuriated my mother because he was becoming fussy too. In reality, I think he's somewhere between me and my sister and the crux of all of this is that we are all individuals with our own tastes and preferences and the food that we enjoy now is not just as a direct result of our upbringing but also our individual taste buds. I am no longer a vegetarian, but still don't eat any meat that you have to chew, sometimes it's easier to declare myself a vegetarian because I tend to prefer the meal options at restaurants and on planes etc. But if I'm completely truthful I am just a fussy eater, which isn't very acceptable in our society for either a child or an adult.

It really dawned on me today when I received a text from a friend inviting us to dinner. My immediate reaction to these types of invitation is dread, not because I won't enjoy their company but because they will stress about me not liking things and feel that they have to make something special for me and that makes me feel awful. I would much rather we just go for drinks and nibbles or go out to the local pub instead where it will be more relaxed and no one has to go to any special trouble.

Then she sent me a text asking if there is anything I don't eat? My immediate thought was "oh god is there anything I do eat that she is likely to make?" Then I feel guilty because I genuinely don't want anyone to go to extra trouble for me. You see for me, you eat when you are hungry, not make a big occasion of it. I eat little and often and can't do big meals, I just pick at them. So I don't like meat, I'm not a big fish fan, as soon as people think vegetarian they serve up mushrooms or aubergines or stuffed peppers, none of which I like!! Now you see where this is going…. dare I say all of this in a text? So I responded with a slightly shorter edited version that still seemed like a book and made me feel awful. I dread to think what she thought when she read it. To top it all, I'm not drinking wine at the moment because I'm convinced it gives me a bad tummy. No I'm not abstaining from alcohol completely but I'm sticking to gin and tonics so is it appropriate to take gin and tonic to a dinner party? I really don't know but I will. I'm not at all relaxed and laid back about this am I!

- **Note to self:** *next time I'm annoyed by my son being a fussy eater I must remember everything I have just written and that it is not his fault.*
- **Second note to self:** *must learn to relax a bit more about the whole eating out thing.*

Chapter Fourteen

Kids Amazing Ability to See Things
From a Different Angle

My 5 year old daughter was in the bath and said "do you know Mummy; we mustn't leave the tap running when we are cleaning our teeth because that wastes water". My 9 year old son was just coming up the stairs when I said "that's right and that's why it's good to have a bath together as well to save water". His response was "did you know that the water levels are rising now and so that means that we should waste water to bring the levels down to save the earth or else the sea will gradually take more and more of the land". "WOW!" I said "that is a very good counter argument for a debate but it really doesn't feel right to waste water when some people have none". "Well, let's give them some then!" he said.

My daughter said to me in the car one day "I don't ever want to get really old!" I thought she was probably thinking she wouldn't want to not be able to do all the fun things like jumping on the trampoline, gymnastics or something like that. But what she actually said was "because then my nose would be really long! Did you know that your nose keeps growing all your life, so imagine how long it would be if you lived to 100!"

"Mummy? Did you know that you shrink when you get older, so you'll be getting smaller while I'm getting taller! Imagine how small you will be when you're 100! And with a really long nose!"

Um Great, I'll look forward to that then!

Chapter Fifteen

From Organising Their Lives to Letting Them Have Their Independence

I don't think my kids do that many activities compared to some but along with all the school activities particularly at the end of each term it becomes a crazy juggling act when we are all already exhausted because it's the end of a very busy term and we all need a break. I finished work today at 5pm, collected the kids from after school club, not forgetting the PE kits because I have to get them washed, dried and ironed ready for tomorrow. My daughter has sports multi skills at the high school with all the other primary school children her age from the catchment area. Then I have to make togas for their school sports day, which has a Greek theme this year, they need them for the day after tomorrow and I will need to make myself one as well because I have offered to help. I'm taking a half day holiday off work and I love being involved at school but then the pressure will be well and truly on at work to get everything done in the time I have left before taking the first 3 weeks of the summer holidays off. Then my son has a cricket tournament all day Friday followed by his first cub camp.

I have the full kit list of everything he needs to take and I've been shopping already so I feel quite organised,

I just can't believe how fretful I feel and my stomach is churning at the thought of him going. I know he'll have a great time and he can't wait but I will miss him so much. I mustn't let him see my worries, no crying in front of him! I do need to send an email to the cub leader though just to make sure he is aware of his health issues – asthma and hearing problems at the moment. Gosh! The cub leader seems so young, would he cope if there was a real problem? Stop worrying! I have to keep saying to myself and focus on what needs to be done, label everything and start packing his rucksack. I'm so apprehensive, he's so excited! I finally sit down at 9.30pm, I haven't stopped all evening and haven't managed to label all the kit or pack it, that'll have to be done tomorrow.

Just two nights until my son goes on his first cub camp and I can't help feeling really strange but trying so hard to be jolly and happy about it. We have packed his rucksack together so that he knows where everything is, ticking off the kit list as each item went in. When we were doing this he looked at me and said "aren't you coming with me?" This was the first time he had shown any kind of apprehension and it took everything I had not to burst into tears there and then. I stopped myself and took a deep breath and explained that parents aren't allowed to come. I felt guilty, had he not understood that going to cub camp was on his own with other cubs and leaders or was it just an innocent question because I have involved myself in so much of his life. Then it dawned on me that maybe he meant was I not coming with him to drop him off at the camp. I decided a few days ago that it would be best if his Dad dropped him off because I would probably cry and keep asking whether he was OK which wouldn't give him the confidence he needs and would be highly embarrassing in front of his friends.

He's been gone about an hour and I just went into his bedroom to draw the curtains. I'm missing him already, it'll be the longest he's ever been away from us and we can't even speak to him on the phone because there are no mobile phones allowed and no contact unless it is an emergency. I know he'll have a great time and it'll be good for all of us. Letting go is one of the hardest things and I can't imagine how I'll be when they leave home, so each little step is good for us all (I just keep saying that to myself).

I'm so excited now because it's time to set off and pick him up from cub camp. How different this feels to the dropping off, this time we all get in the car, all looking forward to seeing him and wondering whether he has enjoyed himself. As we walk across the camp site towards his troop and I catch sight of him I just want to run up and give him a big hug and bring him home but I have to hold myself back, mustn't embarrass him! He's with all the other cubs and leaders and he looks absolutely exhausted. Then we have to wait and watch while they have all the awards and closing ceremony. It's fantastic, a sing a long, prizes, thank you's. I'm so proud of him and it's taking all my strength to keep the tears from my eyes, the corners of my mouth keep going and I keep trying to turn it into a smile, it must look more like a grimace! This has been one of my first experiences of having to stand back and let him be independent, I'm sure it's always going to be difficult but it is important for his development into teenager and adulthood and my development into a Mum of older children.

Chapter Sixteen

I am Not a Domestic Goddess!

God I hate house work, it doesn't come naturally to me at all. I can probably blame my Mum for that one, maybe it's in our genes, and now that I am older and have kids of my own, I realise that it was a good thing that the house was always way down on the list of priorities for my Mum, who was also a working Mum. In fact, give my Mum due respect she worked full time from when my brother started school. I remember my Dad was made redundant and my Mum was completely determined that she would work full time and earn good money to ensure that we would never have to sell the family home. My Dad has always worked even now at the age of 70 but as a self-employed consultant, since being made redundant, so I suppose that moment took the security away and my Mum needed to know that the house was secure. It has always been very important to her in the sense of having a large house with land and the freedom that gives, not in a show house way. I remember being a little embarrassed as a teenager bringing friends home because the house was pretty messy but actually I was mostly proud of our open house policy where everyone was always welcome, whatever time and could always stay for a meal, sleep over or just chill. There was never any pressure about keeping the place clean and tidy.

These days people seem to have become obsessed with having a show home like on all of those make over programmes, does this really make you happy? Is that really a particularly important thing in life? Will "always had an immaculate house" appear on their gravestone? Is it something to be proud of or is it a sign of a lot of wasted time and energy? The obsession with material possessions and celebrity lifestyle has got completely out of hand, what are we teaching our children? I would like to think that I am keeping things in perspective, like a list of importance of what we should spend our time doing and spend our money on. You don't need 'things' (like a new kitchen) to have fun, we can have a fantastic time down the park just playing tig, going for picnics, going for bike rides (OK you do need bikes for that!). But really, being healthy and having lots of fun together as a family is much more important than having the 'perfect' house filled with lots of expensive stuff. The tread mill of work, to earn money, to buy things. I just want to slow it all down and enjoy life with my children and my husband and our friends and family. The only little flaw in this is my desire for travel, particularly to Florida, where we have friends and we all love to go and visit them and have a great family holiday, which obviously costs a pretty penny!

Chapter Seventeen

Cultural Lies to Make Childhood Magical – is it Ever Right to Lie?

The Tooth Fairy

My daughter just lost her fourth tooth and she wouldn't go to sleep with the tooth in an envelope under her pillow. She said she wanted to keep it and look at it again in the morning. So I said OK but I had a feeling that something was wrong and she was obviously thinking about this very deeply. Was she frightened of the tooth fairy? We have a beautiful book all about tooth fairies and I thought it made it all feel very magical. Then I can't help wondering to myself why do we have to tell these lies to our children? We feel we have to go along with it all because if everyone doesn't then the magic and mystique will be gone for all children. But if it worries our children or makes them feel frightened is it right?

The next night she decided she would sleep with it under her pillow so I thought phew! She's OK, maybe I was thinking too deeply. 6 am the next morning she came into our bedroom crying her eyes out and saying "I want my tooth back". She was really sobbing and in that moment I had to think what to say when I was still half asleep. I said "I'm sure we could get it back, do you want to give the pound back?", still sobbing she said "yes, I don't want the money, I want my tooth but how will you be able to get it back? The tooth fairy's got it now!" In this moment I decided to tell her the truth and felt awful for going along with the lie in the first place. I have always said to my children that it is important to tell the truth and shouldn't I be leading by example?

I always keep all the teeth so I showed her where they were. She was so pleased to see all her teeth again. She said "are you keeping them for me for when I'm older?" I said that she probably won't want them when she's older but that I am keeping them forever because they are very precious to me, along with the first piece of hair cut off, the hospital band and hospital tag. I also keep their first shoes and a couple of their first outfits.

"Will you really keep them forever? Until you die?"

"Yes, I really will but if you would like, you can have them after that".

Oh boy! I hope we don't have anything like this at Christmas!

Part Two

Have We Made it?

Chapter Eighteen

I Think We've Made it!

Oh my God! I think we've made it without any irreparable damage to our marriage. The kids are now 12 and 8 and since our son started high school in September there has been a much calmer air around the house. He was ready to go to high school and had completely out grown primary school, finding it very boring at the end. He has taken to high school so well; he loves all the different subjects and is even taking the homework in his stride. He has become so much more independent because he walks down to the bus stop, leaving the house at 8.00am and then walks back from the bus dropping him off, getting home around 4.30pm. He even has a key for the odd occasion when I haven't quite got home, although I would never leave him for long yet and Mum is normally in and only 4 doors away. After he has left for school in the morning, my daughter and I calmly get ready, I drop her off at school and go straight to work. It has at last become the peaceful mornings that I longed for. I am still doing all the breakfasts and getting the lunches ready for the day but because we don't all have to be out of the house at the same time it just all seems so much easier.

I can't even begin to tell you how relieved I feel that we have got through the baby and toddler and just starting school phases. Much of it seems a blur and there have been so many occasions where I have felt that I just couldn't cope any more, that I was losing my mind or that my husband was completely losing the plot (mostly at the same time as I was struggling to cope). We seemed to be operating at odds with each other, vying for time and importance of job instead of working together as a team. It sometimes seemed more of a tag team event than a family growing together, you know the scene, I'll drop off today and you pick up, then you take to cubs while I take to dancing, then the party on Saturday, then you're away for work and I have a work night out when you get back etc.... The one thing that I have always made sure of though is that we had one night out a week together, even when I really didn't feel up to going out and could just as easily have stayed in but I truly believe that this kept our marriage alive and as the years have gone by we enjoy our night out more and more.

October 1st 2011 – it's the hottest October day ever.

We've just had a glorious day in the garden, enjoying this unexpected October sunshine. We got the pool back out that had been packed away for the winter. The kids have had friends round and the girls have just spent endless hours in the pool having fun while the boys have been doing what boys do, Xbox, nurf wars in the garden, messing around in the shed.

Then we met our friends at the pub, with their kids and we all get on so well, have so much in common, with kids the same ages. The pub has a fantastic garden area, with trees to climb and big areas of grass to play ball games on. The kids play together so well and we are all relaxed. I occasionally catch them out of the corner of my eye, hitting each other with bats (the soft kind so that's OK!) but they are all doing it equally and equally enjoying it so 'hey' I've learnt to turn a little bit of a blind eye in these situations, I didn't used to be able to but the new me is trying to be a little more relaxed and laid back. No one's crying, they're all having fun. We're having a nice drink in the sunshine with our friends, enjoying adult company and conversation, WOW! We have finally come full circle back to what we enjoy doing. Or is it just the lull before the storm of the teenage years?

As I look around at my husband and our friends, I can't help noticing that we are all showing signs of age. I could never imagine myself getting old but just lately I have occasionally caught a sideways glance in the mirror and noticed my neck is no longer my own but one of an older woman. As I look around, I notice that the others have similar necks. I remember an older friend once saying to me that you get to 40 and think this is great, I don't feel or look much different to when I was 30 but then each year after 40 there are little signs that appear to show you that you are getting older and are no more immune to the signs of ageing.

Do I care? I'm not really sure! I have a relieved feeling of getting through the children's younger years without any serious consequences to my mental or physical health and with our marriage still intact 'no collateral damage!' so to speak. I am starting to feel calmer and understand that what is important to me is important and not to be pushed aside. It's not just all about the kids and my husband and keeping them all happy. I'm reading a lot more now and enjoying the peace and the 'me time' that I can have. I'm definitely not going to rush back to full time working or increase my hours, although we could do with the money now that our family holidays are so expensive and we all enjoy them so much. I can't believe that on a flight the kids are classed as adults from the age of 12 and for theme parks in Florida they are adults from the age of 10! No, I am going to use this time to reassess me and what I want to do. To keep the work life balance I have and not put more pressure on myself. Getting older can be a good thing because I do know myself better now. I will enjoy this time and use it to equip me for the next phase in our adventure as parents. I am looking forward to having a bit more freedom to do what I want to do and hopefully some great adventures together as a family and as a couple when the kids don't want to come with us anymore.

Chapter Nineteen

Just When I Thought it was Going so Well!

I've had one of my busiest years ever at work and it has been incredibly stressful. I feel that I couldn't have done any more or worked any harder. I've literally got to work each day that I work and worked at 100 miles an hour without any breaks and struggled to get away on time, many times having to ring my husband or my Mum to pick up the kids because I just couldn't get away. Throughout the year while I was working like this and so were pretty much all of my colleagues I felt that I was appreciated for working so hard and for me that is reward enough and keeps me motivated. The air at work has become so tense now, everyone seems so stressed that it no longer feels like the business I am used to. I have been given direct feedback by a senior manager that in his opinion and he believes this to be the company's view you can't do my level of job part time and I should work longer hours. My stomach is churning, I can't sleep at night because I am such a conscientious worker, I have never been directly criticised for working part time before and have been with the business for 18 years and worked part time very successfully for 12 years. I feel like there is an ulterior motive going on here, I haven't changed the way I work and in fact as I have already said I have worked harder than ever in the last year. I live the company's values of freedom, responsibility, mutuality, quality and efficiency and that is how I have successfully balanced being a Mum with having a great career. I will not be forced to change, not now, not ever!

I have been allowed to be the best I can be at work while having the time at home with my children as well. This is me and this is vital to me. This is what I feel is now being threatened as they put more and more pressure on my role which is then not going to be achievable in 3 days a week.

The thing is, some people need the assurance of fitting in, security, being the same as others to be able to compare themselves to. For me it is important that I have the freedom to be me and my values are respected and I am appreciated for being me, even if that is different to others, I see that as one of my strengths. This is how I perform to my best and have given all I can to the company. When what they are asking for is challenging my values and encroaching on my role as a Mum, I will stand up and fight. The inner turmoil that I am feeling is counterproductive though and now I can't perform to my best either at work or at home, so what do I do?

Is this the end of the line for my wonderful work/life balance that I have had for so long? I am not prepared to sell my values! Therefore I will not work more hours and whereas I would have worked harder and harder to do the job within the hours, I will now stand tall and challenge the real feasibility of what they are expecting in 3 days a week. I would love to just leave now that it has made me feel like this but as with everyone, finances do have to come into it and it is never as simple as that. My husband came up with a great suggestion last night (after many others like start looking for another job with other local businesses, my reaction to that one was no way, I don't want to be owned by another company!) What I really want is my freedom and the weight to be lifted from my shoulders so that I am not thinking about work even when I'm not there. I want serenity, I want peace, I want love, I want to be a Mum to my children and be there for them when they need me and when they don't need me, I want to be fulfilling my dreams and to be in control of my own destiny. Now that really is getting carried away isn't it! I probably need to break that down into something a bit more realistic and achievable. Anyway, my husband's great suggestion was that if they are putting more and more into my role and I believe that if they ever replaced me it would be with a full time person then why not suggest a job share. Actually I have never liked the idea of sharing my job because I like to be fully responsible for what I am doing but thinking about it now it would take the pressure off when I'm not at work. Some work would still be done when I'm not there and when I'm on holiday, which would be a real benefit. I could actually work less hours rather than more and have more time at home.

Having an alternative option in my head to leaving and the financial hardship that would cause the family has helped me to sleep at night again but I have decided to take charge of my life and read the Paul McKenna book 'Change Your Life in 7 Days' because right now it is the weekend and I can have some sanity and time to reflect on what is important but when I go back to work on Tuesday the chaos is likely to resume and I need to gain some control over my emotions and develop a game plan for my future.

After reading day 1 of the Paul McKenna book I think

my problem is that I already know my 'inner self', my ideal me is a calm, successful mother in full control of her own destiny. Spending my time working well on something that is self-fulfilling that I am good at and only while the children are at school and then switching off from it and being there for the kids when they need me. I'd love to walk to and from school every day instead of always being in a rush. I'd love to turn the whole pace of life down but still be successful. Is that achievable?

Day 2 of Paul McKenna and he says to remember how you felt when someone you respect last paid you a complement. I thought and thought and truly racked my brains but literally couldn't think of a single example when someone I care about last paid me a complement. That's really sad isn't it! I burst into tears over breakfast when I tried to tell my husband. I'm in a terrible emotional state now and just can't think straight at all. Oh dear day 2 really hasn't helped me Paul! I feel an absolute mess and what was just a problem at work has become a problem at home as well.

OK, I'll rally myself and try more positive thinking!

Terrible night's sleep again, everything going round and round in my head from 4 am onwards.

I'm not at work tomorrow so I must try more positive thinking; I need to be in control of my emotions especially when I'm back at work.

Day 3: I'm having a better day today because I'm at home on my own, I've got a whole list of stuff to do and I'm enjoying the peace and calm. I'll try Paul McKenna day 3. Good so far, making me smile. Frame everything with a positive angle. Then get text from friend at work (nothing particularly relevant) and strange hostile feelings are rearing up inside me again and I really don't know why. Think positive! Come on focus….

Why is it so important for me to have a successful career? Isn't being a Mum the most important job in the world? Where did we lose sight of the importance and stop respecting Mums for being Mums? How can the next generation grow up to be well rounded, responsible, respectful, content adults without the nurturing care of a mother who has time for them?

Maybe the real problem is that I know what I want and what is important to me but I think I can't have it. So I need to work out how I can have it.

Number one; I want to be a Mum, number two; I want to slow down the pace of my life and enjoy every moment with my family and have some calm time to reflect, write, read and think. I love my family so much it hurts sometimes and I cry at the slightest little things but I think I am starting to understand why. I think I have pushed myself too hard, trying to be good at everything. I think I need more time to enjoy the wonderful family I have and more time for me to think. Work is no longer as important to me when I list what I want in life, what I love and how I would want to be remembered. I would want people to remember me as a positive, fun, calm, thoughtful person hopefully with a bit of wit and intelligence. I would like to read more, to learn more with my children, to have time for hobbies without them becoming a chore that there is never time to do. To read, write, sew, learn and communicate. OK Paul, you are only really telling me what I already know but you have helped me to get it straight in my head. I know what my goal is; now I need to achieve it.

Day 5 of Paul McKenna has completely solidified my belief that all my recent illnesses including reactive arthritis and spontaneous keloid scarring (occurring 30 years after the original trauma) are actually the result of stress and the impact it has on my own immune system. I am trying so hard to be fantastic at work and at home that my body is no longer able to cope with the continual stress that I have and my immune system keeps attacking itself. I absolutely agree with his theories on stress causing physical illness and I am even thinking back to how stressed I was 6 years ago when I suddenly had a severely prolapsed disc, indenting my spinal cord at the lower part of my neck. I was in such excruciating pain that did seem to come on all of a sudden but when I think back I can remember the signs. I was really struggling to use the mouse at work with pains shooting up my right arm causing me to constantly put my arm up in the air to alleviate the symptoms but I never stopped, sometimes I would swap the mouse to my left hand but still never took any time off. Until the pain was so bad I was sweating, I didn't know what to do with myself, I was losing strength in my right arm and couldn't do even simple things like making a cheese sauce anymore because I couldn't stir, I couldn't even spread bread and writing was really difficult. It was so bad that even sitting in the car was excruciating because every tiny bump went straight to my spine causing more pain. I had to walk around holding my right arm up, as though it were in an invisible sling, to alleviate the pain that used to be shooting down my arm and continually in the top of my wrist. I finally went to the doctor and he said I must take anti-inflammatory tablets and pain killers and take at least 2 weeks off work. I went to a physiotherapist immediately as well but this was the point where I realised that it may not be as easy as a bit of physio and a few tablets to solve my problem because the physio said there was nothing she could do for me because she didn't want to risk making it any worse and that I must go for an MRI scan as soon as possible. In hindsight, if I'd listened to my body sooner it may not have been so severe. I didn't even manage to wait a week on the anti-inflammatory tablets and pain killers without going back to the doctors; I knew I needed a specialist. Amazingly my doctor got on the phone straight away and got me an appointment with a consultant within a few days. To cut a long story short when I went for the results of the MRI scan the consultant told me that the scan confirmed a severely prolapsed disc in my cervical spine (at the base of my neck) it was pressing so badly on my spinal cord that the only real option was surgery to remove the disc and fuse my spine at that point. There was risk of paralysis if I did nothing and I was already so weak in my right arm and unable to do so many basic activities. There was also risk of paralysis with the surgery and I remember bursting into tears with the shock of the severity of my problem. Actually needing surgery had truly never entered my head. The consultant calmly said that it could have been worse, it could have been a tumour and with that I tried to pull myself together and just be practical. I kept telling myself that I was lucky because I had private health cover through work which had meant that I got the diagnosis very quickly, I had a great surgeon and I was in the best care.

At this time my daughter was 2 and my son was 6 and I was going to have the operation in 6 weeks' time because I had to have stopped taking the contraceptive pill for 6 weeks before surgery, so it was literally as quick as it could be; no time to think about it, perhaps that was best. That would be the beginning of December and after the operation I wouldn't be able to drive for 12 weeks and I would need to wear a neck brace moulded from my chest to my chin so movement would be very restricted. In those 6 weeks I did all the practical stuff of ordering Christmas presents on line, getting all the Christmas cards, addresses and lists all ready. Worked out the itinerary for the children, who would drop off, pick up, when the activities were etc. all done in excruciating pain, taking strong pain killers which did make me very sleepy but the one thing I never did was think about me or get my head round what was happening to me. I just kept those stress levels going by organising everything, worrying about everyone and worrying about the effect my physical inability was having on my children. I couldn't lift my 2 year daughter and would I ever be able to again? It was heart-breaking and I was very cross about it. I even worried whether I would ever be able to work again.

After the surgery it was amazing, my surgeon waited for me to come round and then asked me to squeeze his hand and I could do it with strength so I knew it had worked. He said it was the largest piece of disc he had ever removed from actually pressing on a spinal cord and I could see the relief on his face that he had done it. Then the really scary thing was the fact that I couldn't even lift or move my head so I had the strength back in my right arm but now I needed to regain the strength in my neck. This is where the recovery from a cervical spinal fusion is so hard because your head is so heavy and your neck needs to be so strong – I was so weak, even the smallest of tasks was practically impossible. I really hadn't prepared myself for this at all but I had no choice but to take each day at a time and do everything the consultant said. My son helped me around the house, picking things up off the floor and putting the washing in but it was terrible not being able to pick my daughter up and really not being able to look after my children on my own. I felt so frustrated, upset and angry with my whole situation. I continued taking the strong pain killers even when the severe pain had gone because they helped me sleep and I struggled to get out of this cycle of trying to do too much in the day and relying on strong painkillers at night to be able to sleep.

Then it was time to go back to work and in a strange way it felt good that I had got through this and I could go back to work and I could be normal again. When I look back now though, the one thing I had never done through all of this was consider my mental health and I actually think that I have been on the edge of a breakdown for years since and this is the first point that I have taken time for me and my sanity. Writing my feelings down really helps.

Reading this chapter of Paul McKenna's has made me truly realise the importance of a stress free existence for a healthy, happy life and I will try my hardest to always remember this and if I am ever having a lapse I will re-read this chapter of the Paul McKenna book, it has been really powerful for me.

Day 6 of Paul McKenna – creating money; this chapter isn't really doing it for me because all the other things I now know that I want are more important than money. The only thing keeping me interested is my belief that money would buy me freedom and therefore the time to be the person I want to be. Actually yet again if you put Paul's advice in your own context it is powerful. I need to focus on getting the debts paid down so that how much I earn won't be ruling me, then I could earn less with the same quality of life and you never know I might even be able to make a bit of money doing the things that I enjoy so much, like writing. I like the idea of working out how much money you need to be able to not work for however long it would take you to start your new ambition and for it to start paying. The only problem being that I want to be an Author which is very tricky to put a time line on.

Do you know what Paul McKenna, I think I'm there. I understand my values better; I know what is important to me and what I want out of life, now I need to set a plan in place of how I am going to do it.

The things I have jotted down while reading this Paul McKenna book are:

- Time is precious.
- Love.
- Understanding: I need to be more understanding with my husband, particularly the times when I can now see that I have been jealous of the fact that he has always kept his freedom. If I recover my freedom, I think I can become a better person.
- I want to be calm, loving, fun, creative and full of ideas and possibilities not stifled by the routine and expectations of today's world.
- Freedom.
- I love this quote: George Bernard Shaw said 'The reasonable man adapts himself to the world; the unreasonable one persists in trying to adapt the world

to himself. Therefore all progress depends on the unreasonable man. Perhaps I am the unreasonable woman, not willing to accept that I must continue with this exhausting expectation of work and looking after the children. I can do a great job with part-time and flexible working hours. I can be a great Mum and wife (the wife bit I don't mean in the old fashioned sense of having tea ready, I mean still be the old fun me, relaxed and good company, not stressed beyond any reasonable behaviour).

- I want to make a difference to other women who feel like me so that they can feel important as a Mum, however they choose to do it.
- I want to have more time for conversation, thinking, reading, writing, Fun, learning and have some real adventures.

Now how will I achieve this?

It did just occur to me that this could be a mid-life crisis!

I read this in a novel by Joanna Trollope 'you can change your situation, but it will be the same if you don't change yourself.' It made me stop and think how true that is and my take on this is to be careful because everything is entwined and the first step I must make is changing myself, have the confidence to be me and be true to my values, be strong and not succumb to 'others' stress being put onto me, keep calm and not take too much on. Then if it still feels right, change the things around me that need to be changed.

Chapter Twenty

New Year's Resolutions

What better time of year is there to look at making significant changes in the way I think, the way I behave and the way I live my life. Let's start a new year as a new me, a calmer, more relaxed me with goals that I can achieve.

I just saw a news report on the BBC about meditation and the 'happiest man in the world' a Buddhist monk who obviously meditates a lot. They have qualified him as the happiest man in the world by doing a brain scan that showed the scale of activity in the positive thoughts part of his brain. I've often thought that being able to meditate must be good for your general well-being and help towards a stress free and more relaxed lifestyle. I must try it! It would surely be good for all the family.

It's the 3rd of January and so far I am going to rejoin Weight Watchers, I need to lose about 7lb so it's not too onerous a task. I have set myself a writing target of 2000 words per week just to try and focus on actually finishing this book because last year I got quite stressed about the fact that I never seemed to have time to write, (the one thing I want to do for me, not for anyone else). 2000 words a week should be achievable and breaking it down in this way definitely makes it less daunting. Now I'm adding 15 minutes of meditation each day – can I do it? Oh and I'd like to do at least 15 to 30 minutes either walking or in the home gym every day. When I say home gym that is a bit of an exaggerated term for what is basically a few pieces of second hand equipment and one new cross trainer that my husband bought me for Christmas last year and I haven't used anywhere near enough.

I don't know, do I just get a bit carried away and set myself too many targets that although each one is achievable when you put them all together it does become too much and yet again I stress myself out that I am not achieving what I said I would.

Right, let's focus on what is my number one priority this year; writing, for once I am going to do something for me and let's face it with the target I have set myself it will only take a couple of hours a week spread over several days so no one else in the family will be deprived as a consequence.

Chapter Twenty-One

Back at Work

I'm back at work now after a lovely long Christmas break that I really needed. I feel completely refreshed with a positive outlook on my life, my new year's resolutions are going well and it all feels good. Work seems to have completely calmed down and I feel really in control. Now I'm thinking what on earth was all that about before Christmas? Was everyone just so stressed and exhausted at the end of a busy year that people were picking at each other? Placing blame, whether valid or not and maybe I was over sensitive to it all. Whatever it was though, it has changed me and my whole outlook of what is important to me and what I am prepared to do and what I am definitely not prepared to do. I am now more aware of the physical result on my health of the undue pressure that work can have and I am determined to stay calm and in control this year and not let work ever affect me so deeply again.

We've had the first whole week back at work and school and I think I've done really well and stuck to my 'new me'. I worked 4 hours on Monday, got caught up on all the emails and got myself organised for the year ahead. I finished 2 hours early on both Tuesday and Wednesday to pick up from school. I took my daughter to a new gymnastics class that she has been wanting to do for ages. It wasn't the right class for her but we have a few more to try and I am determined to find the right class that she can enjoy and make progress in, even if it means travelling a bit further, and I will rearrange my working hours to be able to take her. I have kept up with my new year's resolutions, I started Weight Watchers, I've walked for at least 15 minutes every day and I've achieved my writing target. I haven't been doing very much meditation but all in all I feel great and I think I'm doing really well. I feel much calmer than I can ever remember feeling since having the children. Right now I feel that I am balancing everything well but I must keep remembering what I have learnt and not let my mind go racing off planning more and I mustn't take on any extra work or responsibilities because that could just tip me over the edge and I don't want to go back to that unhappy and unhealthy place ever again.

Now that I've set my new year's resolution targets and I am mostly managing to stick to them, particularly my writing target, I just feel so much more fulfilled. In hindsight (which is a wonderful thing!) I think I had simply forgotten to look after myself, emotionally and physically. By taking my need for fulfilment into account and making sure I have time for me and not feeling guilty when I take that time, I am a calmer and completely nicer person to live with. This seems to be working this time, and believe me I have tried to take time for me before. I think it is working this time because I have declared my targets to all the family and I even have a spreadsheet monitoring my achievement on my writing target, which kind of gives me the OK and then I will not feel guilty when I am doing it because if I stop achieving my goal, I will again feel unfulfilled, frustrated and unhappy.

A happy, fulfilled me makes me a much calmer, happier and more tolerant person and definitely a better Mum, wife and human being.

In my much calmer state, I have suddenly realised that I had allowed myself to be downtrodden and deeply affected by basically one very old fashioned manager who chose to express his beliefs towards the inadequacies of women working part time, especially in more senior roles and put it all on me without any evidence, facts or substance just his prejudices. I now realise he did this without the support, backing or agreement of any other managers in the business and actually this does go against everything I know the business stands for but at the time, in my stressed state, I took it all in. I even remember him saying "how many more years has your daughter got at primary school, then you'll be able to go back to full-time working!" f★★★ off! Excuse my language and I really do rarely swear (this was in my head – not out loud). I am a very strong willed person and cannot ever bear to be told what I should do. Constructive, thoughtful opinion I don't mind but old fashioned being instructed to 'tow-the-line' and conform is not me.

I am now looking at myself and I can't believe how I had become so lacking in confidence, so submissive, so not me! An unappreciated part-time Mum I AM NOT! I AM A STRONG, DETERMINED WOMAN WHO IS GREAT AT HER JOB, fantastic at time management and prioritising and should be valued for that. I must stand up, be me and fight again like I always have. The trouble is, this is what it's like to be a woman with strong beliefs and family values and a need to be successful. It is a roller coaster of working

82

yourself into the ground to then be caught off guard and one thing or one person knock you down, pull your stuffing out and leave you empty, lifeless and unfulfilled because you are already so run down from trying to do it all. You may believe them in your subdued state, you may believe you can't do it and throw the towel in. Well I very nearly did throw the towel in but now I'm standing tall again!

It is not un-ambitious or un-feminist to want to look after your own children. It is however incredibly hard work to be determined to be successful at work part-time and look after your own children, to be there for them when they need you. I actually found it easier when they were babies and they went to nursery 3 days a week. It just seems even more of a juggle when they start school and now they are 8 and 12, I don't want to send them to any kind of child care because they want to have friends home and go to friends' houses and I want them to be happy because I believe that they will achieve more at school if they are happy and relaxed out of school time.

I often think it would be so much easier not to have ambition, to be happy with one's lot but whenever I tell myself "OK, you've done enough, just sit back now and enjoy the fruits of your labour" it only ever lasts a short time before something inside me is saying I need to do more. I need to do something, what is the something I need to do? I need to feel I am leaving my mark on this world, making a difference in some small (although I would like it to be large) way. I am constantly bringing myself back down to earth to remember the pressure I already have of looking after my children and having a career.

Chapter Twenty-Two

Dyslexia

At school drop off this morning the Headmaster pulled me to one side to talk to me about my daughter and said that he was concerned over the disparity between her speaking ability and her written ability and possibly her reading. Although she has been doing well and is about average, he just feels there could be something and asked whether there was any dyslexia in the family. I said that I had mentioned it a few times over the last 2 years but on each occasion I had been reassured that she was not dyslexic, probably because she was achieving average and above average results. My nephew, my sister's youngest, is very dyslexic but also very intelligent and in a similar way was able to achieve average results at primary school but my sister knew there was something wrong and he was getting very frustrated and this affected his behaviour. It was 10 years ago when he was 8 that my sister paid for the private dyslexia test and he came out as highly dyslexic. I remember how stressful it was for my sister at the time and there seemed to be very little support and she had to fight for everything. Now, with my daughter aged 8 and the headmaster approaching me, I can see that this is a different era and I am not for one minute surprised by what he is saying and yet I hadn't pushed for it because my daughter seemed happy and was doing ok. I don't understand enough about dyslexia at the moment so my mission now will be to gain a better understanding and do everything I possibly can for her. It is strange though because people's first reaction is to think that she can't read, well she can read but maybe her development in her reading skills is stunted at this point because of progressing to more difficult books (she is on dark blue spot if that means anything to you). She has already developed her way of reading but I have noticed that I don't think she is fully understanding the context. She can read the words, especially the longer words, she seems to miss or muddle smaller words a lot of the time and now that the books are all text and no pictures I think she can't keep track of what she is reading in her mind. With my daughter though it has been more evident in her writing, her spelling is absolutely atrocious and although she has a magnificent imagination and can come up with fantastic story ideas she struggles to get them written down. She has such a great personality, so creative and imaginative and she is so bright, we must help her to achieve her full potential in whatever way we can.

My daughter had said to me just this morning that she was nervous about writing her story today and I said "there is no need to be nervous you have lots of great ideas, what is your story going to be about?" and she went through the plot, which was brilliant. Now I'm thinking about how she will struggle to write it all down and she will be put off by the fact that the others can get their stories down on paper quicker. She's very competitive and always notices how quickly other children finish their work.

I've started reading up about dyslexia on line and there

are several indicators that I think are relevant to my daughter like obviously good and obviously bad days, unable to spell (oh boy the tears we've had over practicing for spelling tests! It's like torture for her). I've just found the 'Being Dyslexic' website and I love how positive it is, on the home page it says 'being dyslexic is being someone amazing', I so agree with this statement because my daughter has always amazed me with her incredible insight, her creativity, her imagination and the ability to notice everything around her like the changing colour of the blossom on the trees or people's emotions. Then she has her very unconfident times and real lack of self-esteem and I have never been able to understand it but reading things on this website have really helped me to understand her feelings. Reading the bit about basic ways to help your dyslexic child, I suddenly feel quite choked and tearful, this is a whole new era but I must be positive, we will find effective ways to help her develop. I will do everything possible to ensure that she can achieve her full potential.

It says about dyslexics not being able to differentiate between local towns, again this is so true, she never knows where we are but then I have no sense of direction whatsoever so I can sympathise with that one completely. Another quote from the website: 'She will have many disappointments but learn to live with them' I can see now that this is what she is experiencing and she constantly compares her reading ability, her writing and spelling ability to her friends and is upset and I know that this affects her confidence and her self-esteem and yet, as I have already said, she is doing well at school and achieving at least average and above but I think deep down she knows that she isn't achieving her full potential and this creates a frustration within her. I know for some children this frustration then manifests itself into bad behaviour in the classroom, luckily that hasn't happened and she is working really hard so I am very hopeful that with the right help now she could start to feel less frustration and be happier with what she is achieving.

I feel upset that this will now be a challenge for my daughter for the rest of her life but the wonderful positive outlook on the 'being dyslexic' website has made me more than ever appreciate and want to celebrate her gifts because she is a gifted child and if we can help her to find the right ways to cope with and overcome the difficulties she will face I know she will have a great life.

I am adding this note two years after we first discovered our daughter's dyslexia as a recommendation to any parents out there with dyslexic children.

Our daughter took the dyslexia assessment with our local education authority and it confirmed our beliefs and the areas in which she is particularly affected and also highlighted areas that are absolute strengths for her, which gave us a real positive to talk through with her as well.

Then we took her for the colourimetry test. She started by using coloured overlays to help her read and we bought special coloured exercise books for her to write in because as I have said, her writing, particularly spelling, was more affected than her reading. We also found a private tutor, with the aim of building her confidence because at this point she was at rock bottom.

The real breakthrough and magical moment came when we got her a pair of glasses with her personalised coloured tint (determined by an in-depth colourimetry test at the opticians). She loves them, they are really cool and they work. She is truly excelling now in everything. It's an absolute joy to see her with confidence in herself and her ability again.

Chapter Twenty-Three

Fate

'Something that unavoidably befalls a person; fortune'

I believe in fate and see it as a positive thing, even when something that seems negative happens there is normally a reason and it may just open the door to the next opportunity or make you a stronger person. I believe everything happens for a reason and one thing leads to another and always try to look for something positive even if that means digging very deep inside to find it. We become the people we are through the good and bad experiences in our lives and as long as we can learn and grow through all our experiences we become wiser, well rounded human beings.

Fate brought me into contact with a fantastic private tutor for our daughter and I'm sure that she will make the world of difference to her achieving her full potential in life. There is no way that I could teach her no matter how much I want to help her, it just doesn't work well. It becomes like a battle ground and she doesn't respond well to me trying to teach her. I've tried all different techniques including bribes/ rewards but have realised that she does so much better having a private lesson with a skilled and inspirational teacher. We will stick to reading together, which we absolutely love, we're reading Michael Morpurgo's 'Shadow' at the moment and it is an absolutely fantastic story, my daughter will read a page or two, then I'll read a few pages and some nights I just want to read on and on and before I know it it's past nine o'clock!

There is something I remember reading some time ago about 'friends for a reason', 'friends for a season' and friends for a lifetime and this came into my head because of the lovely new friend I met at the gymnastic class that I found for my daughter and she was the one that introduced me to the wonderful private tutor, who I would never have found without her; it's just truly amazing when these things happen, it was meant to be! When I look back at my life I can see that friendships come and go and move on, never falling out but maybe moving on because they have served their reason for both parties. You can have fantastic short stints of fun, work friends come and go, baby friends, fitness friends, slimming friends etc. then there are your lifelong friends, who will always be your friends no matter what, no matter how long it's been since you last saw them. They may come and go throughout your life but they will always be your friend.

Chapter Twenty-Four

Taking Time Off from the Routine

Having children later in life does of course mean that your parents, their grandparents, are that much older. My Mum has been a wonderful help to me, when they were babies she looked after them one day a week, which meant I had one less day at nursery to pay for and made it financially feasible for me to work part time. Then she has always picked up from primary school at least one day a week. My parents only live 4 doors away and have always been available for babysitting. All of a sudden though and it literally feels that sudden, they seem to be having health issues that they struggle to recover from. They seem tired and not as able to think clearly or manage multiple activities or thoughts. They now need me to help them make decisions, to help them understand the tablets the doctors are prescribing, to go to the doctors with them. My children are only 8 and 12 and I find myself having responsibility for my parents and my children and I am feeling the pressure. I feel that I want to encourage my parents to keep their independence by not just making decisions for them or doing things for them but by helping them to do things for themselves. I am trying to help them keep their confidence that they can do things and only come to me when they really need my help. I'll always be there for them but I would like to keep the parent daughter relationship for as long as possible and not replace it with carer to older parents, not yet anyway! This is the double whammy that truly sucks any time left for me into a vortex forever.

I can feel the pressure building again now as I think about how I am going to cope in the summer holidays, I don't feel I can expect Mum to look after the kids even though it would only be for 2 days a week for the 3 weeks we aren't away. Mum has said that she will but I can tell by the way that she said it that she is concerned. She is waiting to hear when she will be having an operation to remove her gall bladder so there is too much uncertainty for her to feel confident that she can look after them. Also Mum and Dad are planning to be away for the last two weeks of the summer holidays and they are worrying whether they'll be able to go because of their health issues. I don't feel it's fair for Mum to also have the responsibility of worrying about looking after my kids while I'm working. I need another plan for these summer holidays and I don't want to find alternative child care. My children are very independent (like me) and know what they want to do and what they don't want to do and I don't think it's fair to make them spend their well-earned summer holidays with people and children that they wouldn't necessarily choose to be with, doing things they wouldn't choose to do. Four years ago I asked for unpaid leave to take the whole summer holidays off before my daughter started school. It wasn't long after recovering from spinal surgery and I was so thankful that the operation had been successful, having mobility and not having pain, that the meaning of life was very fresh and important to me and I wanted to spend the time with my children. My manager at the time agreed and we had the summer of our lives. It's time for me to do that again, I want that stress free, relaxed summer of fun again without worrying about who's looking after the children and what they are doing each day. The only flaw with my idea being that my boss has resigned and we don't know who his replacement will be yet so I have to ask my boss's boss who is new in role and doesn't know me that well. It's always easier to persuade someone when they know you and know that they can trust you to always do your best for the business. I've prepared myself and my pitch to ensure that I do tell him how dedicated to the business I am and that of course the time off would come with the caveat of being completely on top of all work that needs to be completed before the summer holidays and that if there is something urgent while I'm off he can call me and I'll do my utmost to come in or deal with it from home. There is a natural lull in my workload through the summer and having been in my role for eight years, since returning from maternity leave after having my daughter, I have been able to mould the role to suit my hours and the flexibility I need. The company have been fantastic in letting me do this and I have always been very determined and strong willed in what I am prepared to do, however the other side of this is that I am a very dedicated employee and I always give 100% or more (if that's possible) when I'm at work so I know the company gets incredibly good value from me. To be able to work with the flexibility of hours that I have, the most important thing is job design and of course businesses don't generally design jobs with this in mind.

Maybe big businesses should employ Mum's like me to design better roles that incorporate more flexibility and in return they could have more dedicated employees who are engaged and able to achieve their real potential. Mum's do make up a significant percentage of the workforce and in my experience businesses aren't getting the best out of them. It is a two way street, a mutually beneficial way of working, with the company being so flexible with me I am prepared to give so much more in return. I never just 'clock my hours'. My time is always productive or else I'd rather not be there, I have far too many other things that I could be doing.

So, having presented my case in a meeting with my boss's boss, he is fantastic and agrees in principal just needing to check with his predecessor and my boss who's leaving. I can't express what a relief it is and how excited I am at the thought of another summer with my kids. I will work so hard to make sure work see that this can be an advantage for them as well as for me because I will be so refreshed and full of ideas when I return. The other way to look at it is that it saves the business money because I won't be paid during that time. I've said many times now to my husband and my friends that as long as the business keeps saying yes to my requests, I'll be there, more committed than ever because I have the balance I need. I must remember never to be afraid to ask, if you don't ask you definitely don't get.

I am a bit unique in the business, there aren't lots of women working like me so why is that? Is it just that they don't ask? Or don't know what they want or what they could have?

Do businesses realise the incredible commitment and

hard work and the hour for hour value for money they get in return for giving this kind of flexibility? For example, working part time I rarely take time off for doctors' appointments, dentists appointments or even when I have needed to see specialists, I have always tried to have the appointments in my time and most often if I'm going to be ill it's in my time, I rarely take time off sick. So contrary to popular belief that Mum's working part time aren't as dedicated to their work, I would say that I am more dedicated for the time that I am at work and I try to balance my whole life so that when I am at work I can always deliver my best.

I am a feminist at heart but I don't want a man's job at the same pay under the same conditions. What I want is to prove that I can do a fantastic job working part time and flexible hours so that I have the time to look after my children as well. Who invented working 5 days a week, 8 hours a day? It surely wouldn't have been women because we can always see many alternatives that can work just as effectively, like I have already said it's all in the job design and maybe if more women were given the power to design the jobs there would be more variety of working hours available in successful jobs – not just the lower levels! Even with the great job I have with a huge blue chip company, I am completely tied to my role with basically no chance of promotion with the same hours of work so my career is stunted because of my requirement to work part time, that is where this is very wrong and the feminist comes out in me. Will it change in my lifetime? Only if we really stand up and prove what we can achieve without compromising on being a Mum!

Chapter Twenty-Five

My Childhood Memories

I believe that how each of us is brought up through our childhood and teenage years has a major impact on how we behave as adults and how we choose to bring up our own children. The positive and the negative memories influence our personality, behaviour and values.

I still feel like a child at heart, like I have never made the full transition to adulthood. How did I get to 45 years old and yet still feel so young inside? I often feel like I am masquerading as an adult and I am not very convincing as a figure of authority. Do most people feel like this? I'm sure that my parents were complete grow ups before they were out of their teens. They always seemed old before their time but I think it was like that for their generation, there was obviously much more hardship with rationing post war and extremely high expectations of adult behaviour from a very young age.

Falling off my bike is the most significant memory of my childhood.

When my best friend came back to stay with us in the summer holidays when I was 12, I remember being so excited about it and planning what we would do. I really wanted to take her to Bottesford, the village where I went to High School and I remember now planning to go and visit (or accidentally bump into) a boy that I really fancied. I also remember feeling guilty because I had been 'seeing' another boy who was his friend and it felt a bit like planning to 'two-time' him, of course it was all so innocent but so real to me at the time. The village was 13 miles away so we would need to cycle, I decided to let my friend have my bike and I would ride my brothers Chopper bike, do you remember those? With the large back wheel and small front wheel – pretty cool at the time!

My Mum was working full time and said it would be OK for us to go, so off we set. We didn't get very far, about 3 miles into the journey as we were zooming down the first hill, I remember thinking I'll go for it, so that I can make it up the next hill without peddling, so I took my hands off the brakes and the bike went into an uncontrollable wobble sending me flying over the handlebars and down the very gravelly road on my face.

I don't remember anything else about the accident, I don't remember the impact, I can't remember being on the road, I can't remember my friend coming to help me, It's a complete blank.

The next thing I remember is being in our neighbours kitchen with blood all over me and not able to move my mouth. I felt so sore and yet so numb; I was dazed and didn't know what had happened. My friend told us all that she had flagged down a lorry and after persuading the driver he put us and the bikes into the trailer and drove us home. She said that I was conscious all the time but I don't remember any of it. Our neighbour was fantastic, she contacted my Mum and bathed the wounds she could but knew that I would have to go to hospital.

Then I was in the hospital, I think my Mum took me but I can't really remember. They x-rayed, cleaned me up, tried to remove all the grit from the numerous wounds on my face and arms and did a few stitches on the inside of my mouth but to be honest the lower part of my face was so swollen I don't think they knew what to do. All my top front teeth had been pushed back and were loose; one of my front teeth was broken and had pierced my tongue. My nose was split on the bridge. I had cuts and grazes like burns all around my lips, under my nose, around my jaw bone and cheeks. I had severe grazes on my arms and one shoulder and all my wounds had grit in them. I asked if I could look in a mirror, it was a horrible sight! It wasn't me and I just couldn't believe what I had done to myself!

I remember not being able to open my mouth because the swelling was so bad. I had to take crushed penicillin dissolved in a bit of water through a straw because that was the biggest gap I could make between my lips; it was the foulest tasting medicine. When the swelling in my lips had gone down enough to be able to open my mouth and see my teeth, I had to go to an emergency dentist and he made a sort of cast for my teeth for me to wear all the time over the top of them in the hope that they would re-set in the gums and not fall out. So now I was covered in scabs, still very sore and had a weird thing over my top teeth that I would need to keep on for around 6 months.

I wasn't recovered enough to go back to school at the start of the autumn term and all my friends had been told that I had fallen off my bike. I remember the day I did return to school and I particularly remember the shock on everyone's faces and one friend saying "honestly I thought you would just have a couple of plasters on your face". By this point my scars were really red and it was bad enough that I had swollen, scarred lips inside and outside but I also had a slug like scar just under my nose (that I was later to find out was keloid scarring) and it continued to grow. I also had the 'thing' on my teeth that made it difficult to talk and eat and when I think about it now I was really trying to put a brave face on it all but actually was mentally affected and very down.

The keloid scarring under my nose was still growing so I had to go to a consultant and I think it was every other week I went to the hospital and had injections into the scar to try to stop it growing. The pain was excruciating, injecting right under my nose into the very hard scar tissue and it didn't seem to be making any difference. It was a terrible age to have this kind of scarring, I remember being very unhappy.

When I was 15 my Mum arranged a private consultation with a plastic surgeon because the injections hadn't worked and the appearance and discomfort of the keloid scar under my nose was affecting me mentally. I had surgery to remove the lump and re-stitch the area around my nostril. It was quite successful, only growing back slightly and looked better than it had before once it had healed and the redness subsided.

Chapter Twenty-Six

Being a Strong Independent Woman

The one thing I know that my Mum instilled in me and my sister was that we must always be strong minded, independent women, earning our own money and able to be self-sufficient and she lead by example, completely exemplifying this and being a fantastic role model. I think it was hard for my Mum and my Dad for that matter, to be in touch with the youth of the day and what we were all getting up to, 'sex, drugs and rock n roll', the world had moved on so quickly and so much since my Mum and Dad were teenagers. For them becoming an adult very young was a great achievement for us we were trying to 'find' ourselves and having lots of fun in the process.

I think my Mum was and is a feminist, she never declared as much but she was different to the stay at home Mum's that my friends had. When I look back now many of them appear to have been like Margo in the good life and my Mum and Dad were more like Barbara and Tom, strongly independent and individual and not afraid to stand out as being so. Sometimes that is very embarrassing for a child! Mine and my sisters' education was just as important as our brothers. Mum was always striving to improve herself with Open University and then when the family needed it (to keep the house and lifestyle) she went out and got herself a very good job that meant there would be no more money worries. I do admire her for that; however I can't help reflecting that this was also the time that I lost real contact with my Mum. She became a person always in a rush, bad tempered and stressed. I can't remember Mum or Dad laughing very often when I was in my teenage years, it seems like life just became the juggle of work and us and wasn't much fun for them at all. I can see now just how easily that happens!

Maybe this is why I am determined to be a high achiever at work but only part time, giving me the time to be a good and happy Mum as well – that's the theory anyway! Even that I struggle with so I can only imagine how hard it is when you work full time. You must have to be either superwoman or be able to switch off and capsulize your life into boxes not worrying about one part when you are in the other. I absolutely can't do that even now, my mind never stops thinking of the things I need to do and what I might have forgotten at work and at home.

Of course back in my Mum's day part time working wasn't an option in the kind of office jobs she was doing. It would be awful to have to choose either no job at all or work full time, I'm sure it was a difficult decision because her values needed her to be independent, self-sufficient and be able to help in supporting her family. It wasn't her belief that it's the man's role to be the provider, she needed to earn as well.

We have had to fight for our rights as women employees and thanks to European laws we now do have more real opportunities for part time working. I was very aware of my rights on returning from maternity leave and very determined that I could have a fantastic part time job. Particularly when you work for a large organisation, any requests for part time working have to be given full and proper consideration. I knew that the law was on my side but you do need to be decisive about what you want to do and the hours you want to work and you have the best chance of getting what you want on returning from maternity leave. So that's what I did each time. I worked 4 days a week after my first child and proved that a great job can be done part time and I'm actually saving the company money because they would have paid a full time person to do the same job. It's amazing what you can achieve when you are a determined Mum! During that time I even won a high achievement award, which felt amazing. Then after my second child I requested 3 days a week and have worked that ever since. I have vowed to myself to hang onto my part time working because it gives me the time to be the person I want to be and not to ever let myself be tempted by the fact that I could earn so much more money just by working a few more hours and it would take the pressure off at work but it would put so much more pressure on the other side of my life. Sometimes it is hard but I always remind myself that time IS more precious than money, you never get this time back again and you always spend everything you earn anyway.

Chapter Twenty-Seven

How I am Bringing Up My Children

I tell my children that I love them every day, even when I'm cross with them because they've been naughty in some way. I never use withdrawal of love as a punishment, I always say you know I love you but you mustn't do that etc. I hug them often but never embarrass them in public (try not to anyway!) and I would never let them go to sleep without telling them that I love them. Oh dear I am a bit OTT but I can't help it and I am only expressing how I feel and giving them what I have always needed. I am always aware though that everyone is not as needy of love as I am.

When it comes to our relationship at home I am making a real point of being open with them about sex and relationships (at the appropriate age level of course). I try my hardest to never show any embarrassment and talk as openly and as honestly as possible with them. I always encourage them to never worry about asking us a question and I try to never let them be embarrassed, children are amazing at taking things in a very matter of fact way.

When it comes to children being given their freedom to roam, I am in two minds because I am from the original 'latch key' generation where we were given freedom and responsibility for our younger siblings from a very young age but maybe it would have been better to enjoy more of a coveted childhood for longer. My son at 12 obviously has a key and walks himself to and from the bus to school but I do try to be home when he gets back from school, not to look after him but to be there for him. I firmly believe that as your children get older it is important to be there so that if they want or need to talk they can talk to you, if you're not there, the moment is gone and lost forever. One thing that I do passionately the same as my Mum did is always welcome their friends round and provide food and drinks endlessly, this is their home and I want them to enjoy it and not feel they have to be out of the house all the time.

Chapter Twenty-Eight

*The Meaning of Life – Understanding
Who You Are*

My Mum had a brain tumour at the age of 47, when I was 21. Back then we thought that was it, she would die. Mum and Dad called for my brother, sister and I to be at their house because they needed to talk to us. I remember the room feeling really dark and I felt afraid, I didn't want to know what they were going to say, it was a terrible time but Mum was so strong, even though we all knew that she could die. She made sure that she was super fit before the operation, going for long walks every day. The tumour was the size of an egg but thankfully it was benign and the operation was successful. It took Mum a long time to recover and she was left with a facial palsy, deaf in one ear, memory problems and a serious lack of energy. My Mum has never been able to do as much as she used to do and never returned to work but she is amazing and just keeps going and I think enjoys life more now. I am sure that the stress of her full time working and bringing up three children contributed to her developing the brain tumour, obviously you can never know for sure, but having seen my Mum go through what she's been through I am determined to keep my stress levels down and try to look after myself as well as my children.

I now understand my Mum so much better and I know she is a deeply caring and loving person but doesn't show her emotion in the same way that I do. Mum's way of showing her love is very practical, she is always there for all of us and will always help in whatever way is needed and when she is hurting she hides behind a facade that can often come across as anger but is emotional pain. She is fiercely loyal to all of us and wants to protect us from anything bad happening, she is a real fighter.

Now I've reached the ripe age of 46, I feel that I can finally say that I understand myself, I understand my needs, my expectations in life and what is most important to me. We are all unique and individual and the most important thing is to be happy and comfortable in your own skin. I want my children to be truly and deeply happy and that is much more important than wealth but I do believe to be truly happy it is important to feel that you are able to reach your full potential in life. Try to always see the opportunities not the road blocks, if you don't have enough money to do something you really want to do, look for other ways of doing it, look at all the angles and find a way. Don't spend a life wishing for something or wanting something that you think is out of reach, there will always be a way of reaching it, a different way, be resourceful and your reward will be an even greater sense of achievement.

Chapter Twenty-Nine

How Can We Do It All?

In all honesty, I really don't believe it is possible to do it all. To work full time in a successful and challenging career, bring up your children and have a hobby or two. What we end up doing is burning ourselves out and not doing anything as well as we could, then feeling guilty about the things we should be doing better or the time we don't have that we should be spending with our children. We can compromise and work part time with flexibility of hours to be able to meet all the school commitments and it works for a while but it seems that we then have to accept that our career advancement is stopped and we work harder to keep on top of our work in the shorter time that we are working. We can pay for others to look after our children but for me that has never resonated well because I want to be there for my children, to be a significant part of their lives, to truly understand them and witness their magical moments of growing up, to be the underlying influence in their lives and for them to know that they can always rely on me being there for them.

So we already have the dilemma of how to juggle looking after the kids and working, even if it is part time, then how on earth can we possibly look after our own well-being by keeping fit, having a hobby or taking on something new to challenge our mind or body. In my experience this is always what gives, I start every year with good intentions of doing something for myself but there inevitably ends up just not being enough time in the day or week to really fit it in, without completely wearing myself out.

I did discover one new fantastic hobby a while ago, kickboxing, well it started as a great thing to try because I knew my daughter would love it and the class was open for adults and children to do together which is very rare so I thought we should give it a go. After the first class I was hooked. I felt so alive, so flexible, it was exhilarating and because we were doing it together I didn't have to worry about having someone available to look after my daughter while I went to the class, which is why all other keep fit classes haven't been an option for me.

I did my red belt really quickly along with my daughter and felt amazing, I think I did it for about six months but it was when I was doing my second belt and I felt really ill that I started to realise something was wrong. I had been really careful and told my instructor about my spinal fusion so he always said when he felt I shouldn't do certain moves and I'm not saying that the kick boxing caused it but I did find myself back in the situation of having terrible pain and numbness in my arms again. In hindsight kickboxing probably wasn't a great idea for me but I had been working extra hours with a lot of computer work as well so it is difficult to understand the true cause. When I went to see my Consultant I had a prolapsed disc again compromising my spinal cord in my cervical spine, two discs above my fusion. How and why did it happen again? I tried to carry on and take the medication and do everything carefully but this time it was affecting my whole central nervous system and I just couldn't function as a human being, I couldn't do the simplest of tasks. I took time off work sick and rested (at least I'd learnt that lesson from last time) but in the end needed to have surgery again. I had been so adamant I wouldn't ever have surgery again but when I resigned myself to there being no other option that would give me a functioning body back and to not be on huge amounts of pain killer drugs for the rest of my life, I knew I had to have the operation. There are risks with all spinal surgery and with this operation the risks are paralysis and inability to swallow or speak due to the anterior approach of the surgery. I had faith in my surgeon and yet again it was extremely effective.

Immediately after surgery the numbness in my hands and feet had gone and the pain was different, not all trapped and uncomfortable but more direct surgery pain, which I knew would get better. I took time to recover and followed my surgeon's advice. Gradually I felt my body return to normal with some limitations of course but not in constant pain and the numbness had gone, although I still felt very weak. Recovery from major surgery does take time and I had learnt to be patient with myself.

I am forever grateful to my fantastic surgeon, Mr Mehdian, for sorting me out a second time and have taken this as another valuable lesson in life to listen my body and my own needs. I have to break out of this cycle of burning myself out! My body's reaction to stress seems to manifest as physical illness. I am very aware that I have high expectations of myself but I also have the 'golden handcuffs' of a successful corporate career and it is so hard to break free because the benefits are so great. I am seduced to stay in the corporate world, the world I know so well, by the inspirational events, the sometimes amazing challenges, the kudos of my position and pride in working for a huge global business. All of this along with a fantastic remuneration and benefits package has always enticed me to stay even though I feel it is not good for my health and deep down I have wanted to go it alone, to run my own business for a long time but it has felt important to give my family this security. All of this makes it even harder to do what I now know I must do – leave!

I have always felt I should run my own business, be my own boss, be totally in control of my own destiny but I need the courage to leave what I know so well. I work with so many fantastic people, who are my friends and they are my work family, who I have grown up with. It's always easier to stay with what is familiar but I know that it is now the time for me to break free, to regain my freedom to be me.

My dream for my children is for them to achieve their full potential in life and yet I know that I am not and I have realised this is a reason for my intense emotional moments and inner turmoil. It's finally my time and I'm going to take the chance on becoming the me I know I can be. Break the ties, break free of the 'golden handcuffs' and be in control of my own destiny.

Epilogue

I am now 47, a year post my second spinal surgery, life is good and I have learnt valuable lessons along the way. We are seriously planning a major change in our lives now, to escape the rat race, the juggling and the stress. To slow down the pace of our lives and be in control of what we do and when we do it; a family adventure together to live and run our own business in Florida.

My business will be DIANA Network, I have discovered the wonders of women's business networking groups and how it can be a fantastic way for women to achieve the elusive 'having it all'. Working for yourself but being a member of a supportive, dynamic and fun women's networking group where by helping and supporting each other we can achieve greatness on our own terms. By using all of our contacts and connections to help grow our businesses, together we can do it and enjoy ourselves at the same time. To have that help and support from women who truly understand the challenges of being a Mum and running a business is a vital part for women to start and successfully run their own businesses. From my research so far the substantial growth in women owned businesses is evident in the UK and the USA and I believe this is because women want and need to be able to do it all but on their own terms!